Foundations of Medieval History
General Editor M. T. Clanchy

Foundations of Medieval History

Titles in preparation:

Italy and the Hohenstaufen
David Abulafia

The Medieval Inquisition
Bernard Hamilton

The Medieval Reformation
Brenda Bolton

# The End of the Byzantine Empire

**D. M. Nicol**

HM HOLMES & MEIER PUBLISHERS, INC.
IMPORT DIVISION
IUB Building
30 Irving Place, New York, N.Y. 10003

First published 1979
by Edward Arnold (Publishers) Ltd
41 Bedford Square
London WC1B 3DQ

**British Library Cataloguing in Publication Data**

Nicol, Donald MacGillivray
The end of the Byzantine Empire. –
(Foundations of medieval history).
1. Byzantine Empire – History
I. Title II. Series
949.5′04 DF609



ISBN 0-8419-0644-0



*Produced by computer-controlled phototypesetting using OCR input techniques and printed offset by*
Unwin Brothers Limited
The Gresham Press, Old Woking, Surrey
A member of the Staples Printing Group

# Contents

# General preface

The purpose of this series is to provide concise and authoritative introductions to fundamental developments in medieval history. The books are designed to enable students both to master the basic facts about a topic and to form their own point of view. The authors, on their side, have an opportunity to write at greater length—and with more freedom—than in a chapter of a general textbook and, at the same time, to reach out to a wider audience than a specialist monograph commands.

In the present book, Professor Nicol, who is well known to all scholars of Byzantium, has taken up the great and tragic theme of the decline and fall of the empire. It is a vast subject, open to many different interpretations and with far-reaching implications. When Constantinople fell to the Ottoman Turks in 1453, the sultan became 'the heir by right of conquest to all the Caesars and all the Constantines' and the effect was felt throughout Europe and Asia. To write clearly yet briefly, as the author does, about so complex a period, necessarily requires a well defined approach. Professor Nicol adopts an explicitly Byzantine angle, focusing on Constantinople and eastern Europe as the centre of events. In this way, he fashions a coherent narrative—a considerable achievement in the circumstances—while evoking with sympathy and force the cultural and spiritual revival of late Byzantium.

M. T. Clanchy

# Introduction

The Byzantine Empire was the continuation in Christian form of the ancient Roman Empire. Its capital city was Constantinople, the New Rome, founded in AD 330 by the first Christian emperor, Constantine the Great, at the point where Europe and Asia meet. Its boundaries were those of the Roman Empire until the fifth century, when Italy and the western provinces were overrun by the Goths and other non-Roman or barbarian conquerors. In the seventh and eighth centuries the Arabs and the Slavs took over still more of its territory: Syria, Egypt and North Africa were permanently lost to the Arabs. Greece and the Balkans were temporarily lost to the Slavs. The Byzantine Empire, now effectively reduced to the eastern Mediterranean and Asia Minor, was isolated from the rest of the Christian world. But at the same time it was a more compact and manageable unit than before and its civilization was culturally more coherent. Greek became its official language. Latin ceased to be used or studied, even though its inhabitants still called themselves Romans or Romaioi. The myth of the universal Christian Roman Empire, for all that the Goths, Arabs and Slavs had done to it, was as strong in the ninth century as it had been in the time of Constantine the Great.

The golden age of Byzantium lasted for some two centuries, from about 850 to 1050. It was an age first of recovery and then of expansion, of the reconquest of lost territory from the Arabs and still more from the Slavs. Christianity in its Orthodox or Byzantine form was carried into the Slav and Russian worlds, and with it Byzantine concepts of civilization and law. There was a booming monetary economy; the gold coin or bezant was accepted as the standard of international currency. It was the age of some of the greatest products of Byzantine art, architecture and craftsmanship. The emperors and their people were self-confident to the point of complacency. They were convinced of the permanence of their institutions, of their superiority to other races, especially those in the west, and of their rights as heirs to the Greco-Roman civilization of the past. Their society had taken new shapes and forms and there were many institutions which the Romans of antiquity would not have recognized. The system of administration of the provinces, the nature of land tenure and the recruitment and command of the army were all radically changed; and the influence of the church on almost every aspect of life made for a society very different from that of the ancient world. Yet the Byzantines never cut their roots from that world. Their education was based upon it; their legal system derived from it; and even their Christianity was heavily infected by it. Byzantine civilization was indeed an amalgam of three elements: the Christian religion, Greek culture and the Roman tradition.

The decline of the empire set in about the middle of the eleventh century. The centralized government based on Constantinople, which had held the structure together, began to disintegrate. Much of Asia Minor was lost to the Seljuq Turks. The Slav peoples of eastern Europe were ready to assert their independence. As Byzantium began to decline, western Europe was reviving after its dark age. Westerners, or Latins as the Byzantines called them, took to going on pilgrimages to the Holy Land, and then on crusades. They came and they stayed, carving out principalities for themselves in what had once been Byzantine territory. Their merchants wanted more of a share in the wealth of Constantinople and Byzantine markets. In 1204 they combined crusading with business by capturing Constantinople and dividing the empire among themselves.

The Byzantines never really recovered from the shock of the Fourth Crusade. They won back their capital city in 1261, and their empire lived on for nearly two hundred years more. But it was a very different kind of empire, and its inhabitants had no longer any cause for complacency. The Latins, especially the Venetians and the Genoese, were irremovably established as parasites on the Byzantine economy. The wealth of Crete, for example, passed to Venice, the wealth of Chios to Genoa. The structure and the defence of the empire were shattered; and it could not find the strength to resist the new forces of separatism in eastern Europe and of conquest in Asia Minor. Constantinople could no more fulfil its traditional role of defender of the eastern wall of Christendom against Islam, against the growing power of the Osmanlis or Ottoman Turks who set out to conquer what was left of the empire in the second half of the fourteenth century. Finally, in 1453, its capital fell to them, and the Christian Roman Empire was succeeded by the Muslim Ottoman Sultanate.

This book aims to narrate the history of the Byzantine Empire from the time of its first and temporary conquest by the Fourth Crusade in 1204 to its final and permanent extinction by the Turks in 1453. I have tried to write it from the Byzantine point of view, taking Constantinople and eastern Europe as the centre of events. It would be possible to write a history of Serbia or of Bulgaria or still more of Turkey which would present a rather different picture of the last centuries of Byzantium. It has often proved possible to write histories of western Europe in the middle ages which take no account whatever of Byzantium between the Fourth Crusade and the fall of Constantinople to the Turks. But Byzantium was in the centre of all these historical forces and new, emerging civilizations. It was older than any of them; they drew on its experience even while they were sapping its strength; and it still had much to offer even in its declining years.

To write from the Byzantine point of view entails a Byzantine interpretation of what took place. Byzantine historians wrote their often highly sophisticated narratives in strictly chronological sequence. Emperor succeeded emperor and patriarch followed patriarch. The affairs of their ruling families and of the leaders of their church were of compelling interest to them and their readers and they were convinced that history was a matter of personalities who dominated or were overcome by events rather than one of impersonal trends and forces. This kind of historiography may now be out of date. But one does poor justice to the Byzantines if one does not to some extent accept their own view of the causes of their decline and fall. It is a notoriously complicated story and in so short a span it is not possible to encompass it all. Many facts and events have had to be omitted. The notes on further reading may help to fill in some of the gaps or enlarge the picture. But the city of Constantinople, though less and less able to control the empire's destiny, remains at the centre of it; and of this the Byzantines would have approved.

I make no apologies for transliterating Greek names into their nearest orthographic equivalent. The Byzantines were proud of their Greek language and would have been very unhappy to think that posterity had latinized them. I make no apologies either for being occasionally inconsistent in this matter as, for example, with familiar Christian names such as Constantine or with unfamiliar surnames such as Cantacuzene which, since it still exists as a family name in that form, it would be pedantic to render as Kantakouzenos.

D.M.N.

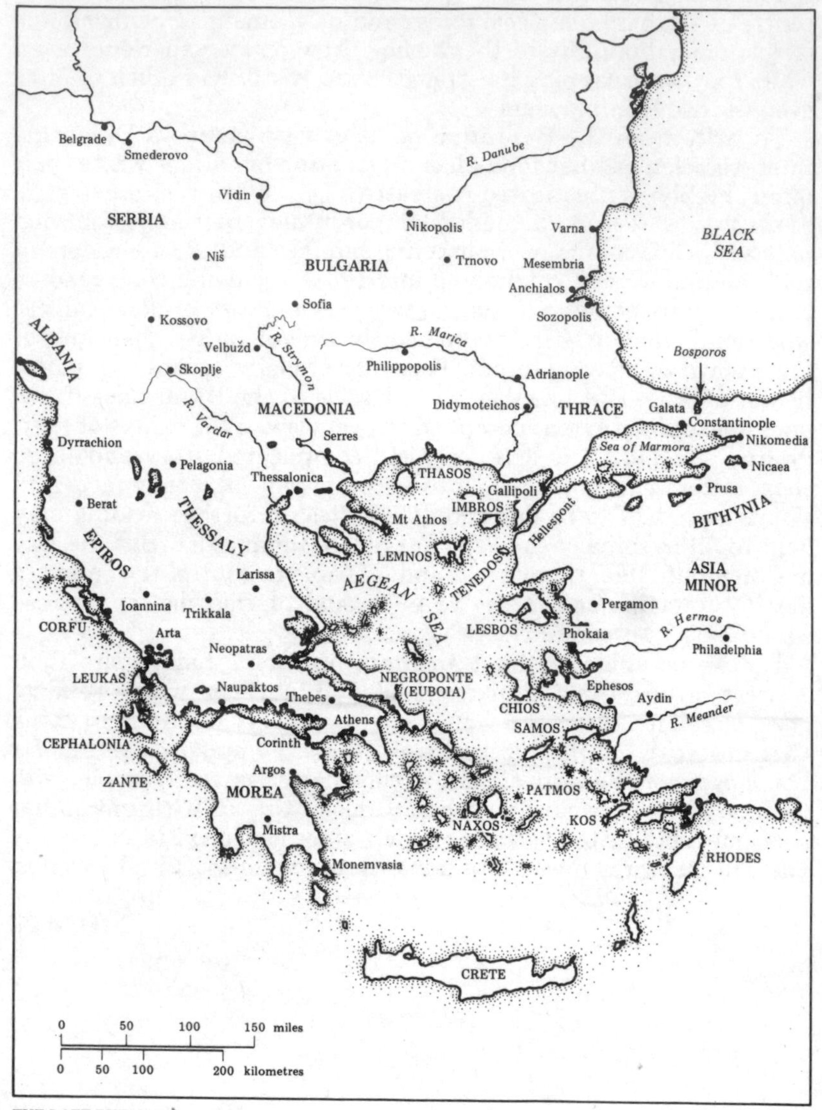


THE LATE BYZANTINE WORLD

# 1 The New Constantine

## The Fourth Crusade and its consequences

About the year 1000 the balance of power in the civilized world lay in the eastern Mediterranean, in the Byzantine Empire centred on Constantinople and the Arab Califate of Baghdad. Two hundred years later the balance had shifted to the Christian west. The crusades had brought new influences to bear on the eastern Mediterranean and new wealth and opportunities to western Europe. The Muslim world, though still strong, was no longer united. The Byzantine Empire, partly through its own weakness, had lost its centralized structure and was in danger of disintegrating into a number of separate principalities owing little or no allegiance to the emperor in Constantinople. The Byzantines had believed that they were God's chosen people, the 'Romans', to be envied and esteemed by all lesser breeds. Their superiority complex had been challenged by the universal ideology proposed by the reformed papacy in the west. The emperor still claimed to be the one true *basileus*, regent of God on earth and visible head of the Christian church; but he could no longer press that claim with much conviction. In 1054 the leaders of the Christian world had angrily responded to the fact that the Greek and Latin sections of the church had gone too far along their different roads to understand each other. They spoke different tongues, they thought different thoughts, and they represented two opposing ideologies. The schism was a first tragic manifestation of the irreconcilability of these opposites.

The crusades brought enterprising Italian traders and businessmen into Byzantine territory. The merchants of Venice were quick to see the wealth to be made in Byzantine markets and quick to exploit the concessions granted to them. A campaign or a crusade to take over Constantinople and put the Byzantine Empire under western management was in some men's minds in the twelfth century. It could be justified on several grounds. The Greeks, it was said, had betrayed the cause of the crusade against the infidel; they stood in the way of its success; and they were in schism from the church of Rome if not in heresy. These half-formulated ideas found their practical fulfilment in the Fourth Crusade in 1203–4. It is possible to argue, though hard to believe, that the Fourth Crusade, which was destined for Egypt, only found its way to Constantinople by a series of mishaps and miscalculations. One of the professed objects of its diversion was to unseat a usurper of the Byzantine throne and replace him by the rightful heir, who had fled to the west to appeal for help and who promised to repay his debt by mending the schism and supporting the cause against the infidel. Only the most naive of the crusaders can have believed that he had the power to do the first or the means to do the second. The Venetians, on whose hired ships the whole enterprise depended, were far from naive. In the end, having forcibly dethroned the usurper in 1203 only to find that his promises were indeed empty, the Venetians and the crusaders felt justified in exacting their own satisfaction. This was no mere collection of unpaid debts. In March 1204 they drew up a treaty of partition envisaging the conquest of the whole Byzantine Empire and dividing Constantinople and its eastern and western provinces among themselves. The eastern Christians and not the infidel Muslims were to be their victims. In April they succeeded for a second time in breaking into the sea walls of the city. This time, however, it was placed firmly under their own management.

The citizens of the 'Queen of Cities' had never before experienced the shame of foreign occupation. But in 1204 the shock was compounded by the behaviour of the crusaders who mercilessly pillaged and ransacked the city for three days. The Byzantines found it hard to believe that these men were Christians in any sense. The worst fears of their anti-Latin fanatics were realized. Those who could afford or contrive it escaped from the horror, the emperor and the patriarch among them. The crusaders solemnly nominated their own emperor and their own patriarch from among themselves and, according to the terms of their treaty, inaugurated the Latin Empire of Constantinople. The pope, Innocent III, was far from pleased with the news of their barbarities. But once the deed was done he convinced himself that the conquest of Constantinople was God's way of winning back the wayward Greeks to the fold of Rome.

The Latin regime lasted for 57 years, from 1204 to 1261. The crusaders successfully occupied and set up their feudal institutions in the south of mainland Greece, in the Peloponnese or the Morea, and in Athens and Thebes. The Venetians, wise from the experience of their merchants, appropriated the major ports and most of the Greek islands. But in the north of Greece and in Asia Minor the Latins failed to establish themselves. There they were denied access or driven out by Byzantine resistance movements which quickly developed into imperial governments in exile, the one in Epiros and Thessaly in northern Greece, the other centred on Nicaea in northwestern Asia Minor. The pretender at Nicaea was the first of the two to have himself crowned as emperor in exile. A third Greek claimant to the imperial title had his headquarters at Trebizond on the southern shore of the Black Sea, though he had laid his claim before the Fourth Crusade. It was an axiom of Byzantine political theory that there could only be one emperor. It was a symptom of the times that there were so many claimants. One effect of the Fourth Crusade was to aggravate the process of fragmentation and decentralization which had already set in a century before. Greeks fought Latins in Greece and in Asia Minor. But the Serbians and Bulgarians, who had proclaimed their independence from Byzantium in the late twelfth century, saw prospects for their own advancement after 1204 and fought both Greeks and Latins. Before the empire was restored to them Greeks were to fight Greeks.

The Byzantine ruler in exile in northern Greece had his moment of glory in the 1220s when he recaptured Thessalonica, the second city of the empire, from the crusaders and was there crowned as emperor. But his 'empire' never developed the solid administrative and economic basis of that established at Nicaea; and in the end, as the Latin regime became ever weaker, the prize of the recovery of Constantinople and the Empire of the Romans was to fall to the Byzantines in Asia Minor. The prelude to that great event, however, was a battle at Pelagonia in the north of Greece in 1259 at which the two contenders fought out their rivalry, a rivalry which was to leave a permanent scar on the body of the reconstituted Byzantine Empire. Two years later, in 1261, the new emperor of Nicaea, Michael Palaiologos, entered Constantinople, which had been delivered to his army almost by accident. The last Latin emperor, Baldwin II, fled to his friends and relatives in Italy, and the Venetians temporarily abandoned their profitable warehouses and dockyards. They would be back. They must have known that the victorious Michael Palaiologos had underwritten his success by doing a deal with their rivals, the Genoese. The rivalry between Venice and Genoa was also to become a running sore in the body of the restored Byzantine Empire.

## The restoration of the Byzantine Empire

Michael Palaiologos, known as Michael VIII, liked to be called the New Constantine. He was the progenitor of all but two of the last Byzantine emperors. His dynasty endured longer than any other in Constantinople, from 1261 to 1453. Yet it was founded on a crime and from the start perplexed by divided loyalties. Politics as they are known today hardly existed in Byzantium. In so autocratic a system opposition or dissidence could, however, be expressed through religious feeling, as it had been in the early years of the Christian Roman Empire or in the age of the iconoclast emperors. It was difficult to tell where religion ended and politics began. Michael Palaiologos was a man of devious character but certain ambition. He had climbed to the top in the small, provincial Empire of Nicaea by offending many of those who had made that empire work. His final offence was to put out the eyes of the boy emperor John Laskaris, the legitimate heir to the throne. This was a moral or religious crime. Michael was excommunicated by the Patriarch Arsenios, who had crowned him. The patriarch's action was applauded by many in the church, but also by many of the lay aristocracy who remained loyal to the memory of the imperial family of Laskaris which had feathered their nests during the years of exile at Nicaea. An opposition party was created. They called themselves the Arsenites in memory of the patriarch. Their minds were on the past, however. In the excitement generated by the recovery of Constantinople the majority of the citizens, who had not seen a Greek emperor in their midst for nearly 60 years, could overlook the crime by which he had made his fortune. The New Constantine therefore came into an empire that was divided. He had enemies at home like the Arsenites and the Laskarids. There were enemies abroad, both Greek and foreign.

The empire in exile at Nicaea had been a small but well ordered enclave, largely self-sufficient and able to hold its own against the declining power of its Muslim neighbours, the Seljuq Turks. In the 1240s its territory had expanded into Europe. Thessalonica was added to it in 1246. Even before the restoration, therefore, the emperor at Nicaea could rightly claim to be master of a Eurasian or Byzantine dominion lacking only its proper capital of Constantinople, the New Rome. Michael VIII worked hard to restore the defences, the palaces and the churches of the city which the Latins had allowed to fall into ruin. Trade revived. The merchants of Genoa eagerly took up the concessions granted to them; and even the Venetians were encouraged to return. But the upkeep of Constantinople, the largest city in the world of that time, drained the limited resources which had been patiently built up by the emperors in exile. The people of Asia Minor, who had prospered under the empire at Nicaea, resented paying high taxes for the defence of Constantinople and the distant European provinces. There were even some who said that the Byzantines would have been better off without Byzantium.

To Michael VIII such sentiments were unthinkable. Fortified by what he believed to be his divine mission as *basileus* of the Romans, Michael planned a vast programme of reconquest in Greece and in the Balkans and a network of alliances and treaties with other powers which would revive the glories of the empire and make it worthy of its capital. He went to war against the separatist Byzantine principality in northern Greece whose rulers, though defeated in 1259, still petulantly refused to recognize him as emperor. He launched a campaign of reconquest against the French princes in the Morea and against the Italians who continued to occupy the Greek islands. He led his armies north into the Balkan mountains to terrorize the Bulgarians back into submission. The extent of his diplomatic manoeuvrings can be illustrated by the marital alliances which he arranged. One of his daughters was given in marriage to the Tsar of Bulgaria, another to the self-styled Emperor of Trebizond, a third to a son of the ruling family in Epiros, a fourth to the Khan of the Mongols of the Golden Horde in south Russia, a fifth to the Ilkhan of the Mongols of Persia; while his eldest son Andronikos, whom he had nominated as his heir in 1261, was married to a daughter of the King of Hungary. This was imperialism and diplomacy on the grand Byzantine scale, a scale which the empire could scarcely now afford.

## The threat from the west: the union of the churches

The most expensive and protracted test of the restored empire's endurance was to come from western Europe. There were several interested parties in the west who lamented the loss of the Latin Empire of Constantinople. There was a movement, backed by the papacy, to recover it by means of another crusade which would restore the Latin emperor Baldwin to his throne and once more unite Christendom by force. Baldwin had taken refuge in Italy at the court of his relative Manfred of Sicily. Manfred had actively supported the Byzantine ruler of Epiros in his struggle for power. He controlled bases in Albania and the coast of northern Greece from which an overland invasion could be mounted against Thessalonica and Constantinople, as the Normans had shown in the twelfth century. The pope would never appoint Manfred, one of the Hohenstaufen 'brood of vipers', as leader of a crusade. But in 1266, with papal blessing, Manfred was overthrown by Charles of Anjou, brother of the pious Louis IX of France, and the western threat to Byzantium at once became a reality. In May 1267 Charles, now King of the Two Sicilies, signed a treaty with the Latin emperor Baldwin and William of Villehardouin, the French Prince of the Morea. It had the approval of the pope and its professed object was the restoration of Constantinople to Latin and Catholic rule.

Within seven years an army was to be assembled to march overland from the Albanian bases which Charles of Anjou had acquired by right of conquest from Manfred.

The emperor in Constantinople could see only two ways to avert this danger. One was by force of arms, which would be unlikely to succeed. The other was by persuasion and diplomacy. The Byzantines had never thought it shameful to resort to diplomacy or even bribery as an alternative to war. Michael VIII knew that it would be useless to approach Charles of Anjou directly, for by the rules of war he could pose as the champion of a dispossessed monarch. The pope was the only person who could put moral restraint on him. It was to the pope therefore that Michael directed his persuasion. He must be convinced that the Byzantines, though in schism from Rome, were prepared to discuss their differences and admit their mistake. It would have needed a more subtle genius even than Michael VIII to sell this policy to his own people. There were still men alive who could recall what the western Christians had done to Constantinople 60 years before, and much of the empire was still under Latin occupation. Most of the Byzantines were in any case conditioned by their baptism and faith to believe that the Roman church was misguided, heretical and a positive menace to their immortal souls.

Emperors in the past had proposed the reunion of the churches as a ploy to win the favour of the papacy and mollify the western powers, but never in such unpromising circumstances. The traditional Byzantine view was that reunion could only be discussed and achieved in an oecumenical council at which the five patriarchs of the church, the bishops of Rome, Constantinople, Alexandria, Antioch and Jerusalem, must be present or represented. Only at such a gathering of the church universal would the Holy Spirit inform the faithful on matters of creed and doctrine. This was far from being the view of the thirteenth-century popes, for whom the definition of such matters lay within the bounds of their own infallible authority. When Michael VIII tentatively suggested to Pope Clement IV that a council might be convened to consider the union of the churches, he was curtly informed that no such council was necessary. He was presented instead with a detailed profession of the Roman faith to which he, his patriarch and his people must subscribe. Then and then only could he be assured of papal protection against his enemies. It was a discouraging start.

Clement IV died in 1268 and for three years there was no pope with whom the emperor could negotiate. He appealed to King Louis of France, begging him to restrain his brother from attacking the Christian Empire; and for a while Charles of Anjou was diverted to helping Louis in his ill-starred crusade in North Africa. But in

1271 he returned to his preparations. The rulers of Serbia and Bulgaria became his allies; the Albanians proclaimed him as their king; and the Byzantine rulers of northern Greece were ready to give his armies free passage through their country because of their hostility to the emperor in Constantinople. In September 1271 the Holy See was at last filled by the election of Gregory X. Gregory had served as a legate in Syria and was known to have the crusade and the union of the churches much in his mind. He soon announced his intention of holding a council in France at which both of these items would be on the agenda. It was to be held at Lyons in 1274. Pope Gregory X was more sympathetic to the Greeks than his predecessors. He hoped that the emperor or his deputy would attend his council. But he had a clear idea about the nature of the union to be achieved; and, as Michael VIII soon discovered, the terms and conditions were to be precisely those laid down by Clement IV. The Byzantines must unconditionally profess their obedience to the Roman church and acknowledge the primacy of Rome.

The emperor was convinced that he had no option but to accept these terms. Charles of Anjou was planning his invasion for 1274. The pope had summoned his council for the same year. It was a matter of urgency to put the Byzantine Empire under the pope's protection. The patriarch and clergy of Constantinople had been aware for some time that their emperor was engaged in private negotiations with the papacy. They had not been greatly dismayed. Former emperors had tried the same trick and the Orthodox faith had not been compromised. But Pope Gregory's proposals forced the emperor to bring the matter into the open and to present his clergy and people with what he saw as a clear choice between submission to Rome or a repetition of the Fourth Crusade. He tried to sweeten the pill by emphasizing that the pope lived far away. He was not likely to come to Constantinople to assert his prerogatives, and the concessions required in the matter of theology were trivial. But the leaders of the church, devoted as they were to the purity of their doctrine, were horrified and the opposition, led by the Patriarch Joseph, was loud and vigorous. The monks, who were always quick to champion the freedom of the church against imperial dictation, condemned the scheme as a betrayal of the faith; and even the splinter group of the Arsenites who had refused to recognize the Patriarch Joseph joined forces with the opposition.

The emperor found some supporters, however, notably John Bekkos, the archivist of St Sophia. Bekkos was a tolerant theologian who, after a spell in prison, convinced himself that the Roman creed and doctrine could be made acceptable. It became possible for the emperor to appoint a small delegation to go to the pope's council in 1274. They were led by the Grand Logothete (or chancellor), George Akropolites, and they took with them a written profession of faith in the terms required by the pope, signed by the emperor and his son Andronikos. The affair was beset by tragedy. One of their two ships was lost on the voyage and the survivors were a month late in reaching France. But finally, on 6 July at the Second Council of Lyons, Akropolites in the name of his emperor swore an oath of obedience to Rome and the reunion of the Orthodox and Catholic churches was solemnly declared to have occurred. The pope was overjoyed. He instructed Charles of Anjou to hold his fire for another year. The Union of Lyons was a spiritual triumph for Pope Gregory and it was a diplomatic triumph for the Emperor Michael. But its long-term consequences were disappointing. No one could pretend that the council had been oecumenically constituted or that any theological or doctrinal discussion had taken place.

After the event the opposition was louder than ever. The Patriarch Joseph had to be removed. He was replaced by the unionist John Bekkos. When persuasion failed the emperor turned to savage persecution of his opponents, not all of whom were priests or monks. They included several members of his own family. Refugees from the terror in Constantinople escaped to Trebizond, to Bulgaria or to northern Greece, where they were welcomed by the defiant rulers of Epiros and Thessaly as martyrs for the true faith. The less fortunate were imprisoned, mutilated or tortured. The combined Greek and Latin crusade, for which Pope Gregory had prayed, never happened. His successors grew ever more sceptical and impatient at the emperor's failure to force the union on his people. If he should fail they would feel justified in sanctioning a crusade against him to be led by Charles of Anjou, who was only waiting for the word to go.

## The threat from the east

For twenty years after the restoration of their city the Byzantines had to live under the constant threat of invasion from the west. Most of their available military strength had to be concentrated on the defence of the western approaches, on the ancient Via Egnatia which ran over the mountains from the Albanian coast to Thessalonica. The eastern frontiers in Asia Minor, where Michael VIII had come to power, were by comparison thinly patrolled. But it was there that the seeds of disaster were being sown. The balance of power between Byzantines and Seljuq Turks which had been held during the years of exile at Nicaea had collapsed with the irruption of the Mongols into Asia. In 1258 the Mongols had captured Baghdad and the Seljuq sultans became their vassals. The upheaval of the Mongol conquests further east caused countless tribes of Turkoman nomads to migrate. They poured into Seljuq territory. The sultans encouraged them to move westwards to the Byzantine frontier. They had no sense of unity, but their livelihood depended on plundering and, as fanatical Muslims, they were fired with the zeal of holy warriors or *ghazis* against the Christians.

If the frontiers had been as well defended as in the days of the empire at Nicaea, the Turkoman invasion might have been contained. But they were not; and in the 1270s the raiders began to penetrate from the upland plains of Anatolia down into the fertile valleys of western Asia Minor. The ancient walled cities were able to protect themselves but they were soon isolated from each other and from Constantinople as the countryside was overrun and devastated. The emperor's response to this new danger was erratic and seldom effectual. He must have rued the day when, to save money, he had withdrawn the privileges formerly granted to military colonists on the eastern frontier. Whenever troops could be spared from Europe they were directed to Asia Minor. The emperor's brother John did valiant work there for a time. His son Andronikos scored some temporary victories in the Meander valley area in 1278. But by 1280 that valley had been occupied by the Muslims. The ancient city of Tralles, which had recently been renamed Andronikopolis, came to be called by its modern name of Aydin, as the headquarters of a Turkoman emir. Similar emirates sprang up in other districts of what had for centuries been Greek soil. Perhaps the Byzantines had been taken by surprise. Their ancestors had been used to living between two fires. But in the thirteenth century, with their territories so fragmented, they could never find the troops to fight on two sides at once; and when the storm of the long-expected invasion finally broke in the west, it was there that their main forces were concentrated.

## Invasion from the west: the Sicilian Vespers and death of Michael VIII

By 1280 it had become clear even to the most optimistic that the Union of Lyons was unworkable. Not only was the emperor, who expressed such longings for peace with the Latins, unable to enforce it. He was also busily attacking their possessions in Greece at every opportunity. He had reason to be apprehensive, since the French principality of the Morea had come under the direct rules of Charles of Anjou in 1278; but the Latins were not unjustified in complaining of his treachery. In August 1280 Pope Nicholas III, who had voiced growing reservations about the alleged union, died. Charles of

Anjou was free of restraint; and in the autumn of that year his army marched inland from the Albanian coast to lay siege to the key fortress of Berat. It says much for the strength and prowess of the Byzantine army that the invasion was repulsed. The commander of Charles's army was taken prisoner and paraded in triumph through Constantinople. Michael VIII was so thrilled that he had the scene of the victory at Berat painted on his palace wall. But the danger was not over. In February 1281 Charles secured the election of a French pope, Martin IV, who had no hesitation in appointing him as leader of a crusade against Constantinople. This time the attempt was to be made by sea, some of the ships being supplied by Venice. The Serbians, the Bulgarians, the French princes in Greece and the Greek rulers of Epiros and Thessaly were all behind it; and the new pope declared his sympathies by renouncing the Union of Lyons and excommunicating the Emperor Michael VIII. Most of the western world seemed to be ranged against him.

But Michael's diplomatic network was still effective and he had friends elsewhere. The King of Hungary was his son-in-law; the Mamluk Sultan of Egypt would lend him ships; and the Khan of the Golden Horde had the Bulgarians in check. Even in the west his agents had been busy. The emperor was in touch with King Peter III of Aragon, an old enemy of Charles of Anjou, and his spies were at work in the very heart of Charles's kingdom fomenting rebellion among the people of Sicily. The 'crusade' was being planned for 1283. But in March 1282 the revolt known as the Sicilian Vespers broke out in Palermo and spread throughout the island. The fleet that Charles was preparing was destroyed and all his schemes were wrecked. In August Peter of Aragon arrived in Sicily and the French were expelled. The threat to Constantinople was at length removed. The Sicilian Vespers would probably have happened sooner or later. The French were far from popular in Sicily. But the timing of the revolt was all important to the Byzantine emperor. He himself boasted that he had been God's instrument in effecting the liberation of the Sicilians. Byzantine gold, still a persuasive commodity, certainly found its way to the court of Aragon and to the rebel leaders in Sicily. The whole truth may never be known. Byzantine diplomacy worked well because it worked in secret. But Michael VIII doubtless knew some of the secrets about the downfall of his most persistent enemy.

A few months later, on 11 December 1282, Michael died. He was on his way at the head of an army to exterminate his still defiant rival in Thessaly. Even in the face of mortal dangers to its survival from west and east, the Byzantine Empire remained divided and disintegrated. Michael VIII, like a true Emperor of the Romans, had put Constantinople back on the map as a world power. He could influence events in Spain and in Sicily. His name was known in Russia, in the Balkans, in Asia Minor, in Egypt and in Persia. He had won back some lost territory in the south of Greece, but he had failed to coerce the Serbians and Bulgarians. Above all, he had been unable to keep order in his own house. There were still many who opposed him as a criminal and a usurper. There were whole areas of empire where his writ never ran, in northern Greece and in Trebizond whose rulers, though chastened, still called themselves emperors. His reign pointed the moral which his successors had to accept, that the empire could no longer be governed as a unit by a centralized bureaucracy. The spirit of local autonomy had grown too strong. Only in the sphere of foreign affairs could the emperor exercise any central control over policy.

Here too Michael VIII had made more foes than friends. His dealings with the papacy had failed to unite Christendom but they had succeeded in uniting many of his loyal supporters with his bitterest opponents. He died condemned by his church and his people as one who had betrayed their faith and their conscience. They might have hailed him as their saviour from western aggression. But instead they counted the cost of their salvation. In material terms it had been intolerably high. Asia Minor, once the heartland of the empire and the source of its regeneration after the Latin conquest, seemed to be all but lost. The frontier of Bithynia, the province nearest to Constantinople, still held. But the Turkish *ghazis* already controlled nearly all the rest. Badly needed revenue and manpower were cut off at source. The strength of the army, which was still substantial, depended on great numbers of foreign mercenaries. There was nothing new in this. It had been the same in the twelfth century; and in the Empire of Nicaea Michael Palaiologos himself had commanded the Latin mercenaries. But it was now beyond the emperor's means to pay for them. Michael had to devalue the gold coinage to make it go further. But it was more in spiritual terms that the Byzantines measured the cost of the salvation which their emperor had brought them; and here they were mainly agreed that the price had been too high. They looked to Michael's son and heir to right the dreadful wrong done to their Christian conscience. The New Constantine died as an outcast and a heretic, excommunicated by the pope, disowned by his own church and detested by most of his people.

# 2

# The old order changeth

## The restoration of Orthodoxy

Michael VIII had left no room for doubt about the succession to the throne. He had crowned his eldest son Andronikos as his co-emperor in 1272 and nominated his grandson Michael as the next in line. Andronikos II was 23 when his father died. He knew that there were many who hoped that the dynasty of Palaiologos would die with its founder and many more who had suffered under his father's persecution. His first act therefore was to renounce the union with the Roman church and to declare himself as the restorer and defender of true Orthodoxy. The unionist Patriarch John Bekkos was dismissed and his now aged predecessor Joseph reinstated. The political prisoners were set free. Those who had stood fast for the faith were now the heroes of the hour. The restoration of Orthodoxy did much towards healing the wounds that Michael VIII had inflicted on his people and to bring back their pride and confidence. The church, in an elaborate programme of purgation, held a number of councils at which the Latinophile collaborators were denounced and the blame for the union was fastened on John Bekkos. He was condemned and exiled.

But there were wounds that went even deeper. Some still refused to accept Joseph as their patriarch and despised Andronikos II, whom Joseph had crowned, as being the son of the usurper Michael who had led them all into heresy. The Arsenite schism within the church took on a new political colour. The problems of the church, which in Byzantium were always the problems of society, were to disrupt the empire for many years to come, and the new emperor was too insecure and, being deeply religious, too committed to be able to control or to ignore them. But at least they were problems native to it, not wished upon it for reasons of foreign policy. A whole generation was to grow up with the comforting illusion that the papacy and the Roman church could be left out of account. The new emperor did not dare to propose that its assistance might be sought even in the defence of Christianity against Islam.

## Changes in society

In times past emperors of strong character and personality had sometimes been able to shape the course of events and leave their stamp upon an age. The successors of Michael VIII were the victims of events over which they had little control. No one proposed a different form of government. The empire was still a divinely ordained institution. But the status of the emperor was changing, as was the nature of Byzantine society. The emperor was no longer the unapproachable, God-like, hieratic figure of the past. His office was shrinking to a more human measure, and his authority was to be shared with members of his family either as co-emperors or as provincial princes with their own domains. Andronikos II was the last emperor who tried to resist the change in this direction. It was too strong to be resisted.

The class of hereditary aristocracy proliferated in numbers and grew in influence. Their power and wealth were based on landed property, much of which they acquired by *pronoia* or favour of the emperor in return for certain obligations to the crown. Such properties, and the revenues which went with them, had originally been non-heritable and inalienable. But Michael VIII had granted their owners the right to transmit them to their heirs and had courted their loyalty by extending their privileges and exemptions. These concessions to the already rich made it increasingly difficult for the class of small landholders to survive; and they bore heavily on the peasants who, tied to the great estates on which they lived, carried most of the burden of taxation. The class of free peasant farmers, which had once been the mainstay of the empire's military and economic strength, was virtually extinct by the end of the thirteenth century. The church was as much to blame as the secular landlords. The great monasteries were for ever adding to their estates and to the number of their dependent peasants; and the church held fast to the tradition that its property was inviolable and could never be requisitioned by the state even in times of crisis. The wealth and privileges of the church and of a few aristocratic families contrasted vividly with the poverty of the peasantry and the urban population of Constantinople.

Andronikos II quickly decided that the empire could not live up to his father's dreams. Economies must be made and commitments reduced. He cut down the size of the army. He disbanded what was left of the navy altogether, in the fond hope that his favoured allies the Genoese would in future defend the empire by sea. He introduced new and higher taxes, some in money and some in kind, payable in measures of wheat and barley. The revenue rose, but it was the people rather than the landed aristocracy who suffered;

and the devaluation of the currency to as little as half its original value encouraged merchants to put more trust in the new gold coinage being minted by the Italian Republics. Byzantium's weakness was their opportunity.

## Exploiters and enemies of Byzantium

The main contenders for the riches of Byzantine trade were Genoa and Venice. The Venetians controlled the islands of Negroponte (Euboia) and Crete together with other valuable market outlets in mainland Greece and stepping stones in the Greek islands. But the Genoese were on the spot in Constantinople with their own commercial quarter at Galata or Pera across the Golden Horn; and they controlled the trade routes to and from the Black Sea. The Venetians had done good business in the crusader states in Syria. When the last Christian bastion fell there in 1291 those markets were closed and they looked north to expand their business in Byzantine waters. Competition between Venice and Genoa soon led to conflict and then to open war, from which the Byzantines were the principal victims. The emperor was forced to take sides and then forced to pay compensation for the damage that both parties had done to each other on his territory. The rivals fought themselves to exhaustion and peace in 1299. But in 1302 Andronikos was bullied into signing a new treaty with Venice; while the Genoese demanded the right to fortify their settlement at Galata in full view of Constantinople. There were Genoese merchant adventurers elsewhere in the empire. Michael VIII had granted some of them the concession to work the alum mines at Phokaia near Smyrna in Asia Minor. In 1304 they seized the offshore island of Chios, there being no Byzantine navy to stop them; and they held it until 1329, thus depriving Constantinople of yet another portion of its revenue.

On the mainland of Greece the outlook was a little more promising. In the north Michael VIII had tried to bring Epiros back into the imperial family by investing its ruler with the title of Despot and giving him a daughter in marriage. Andronikos was thus related to him and planned that his own son Michael should marry the Despot's daughter. The arrangement fell through, however, and she married instead a grandson of Charles of Anjou, Philip of Taranto, who as a result became overlord of the French territories in Epiros and Albania. This might have been matter for concern if Philip had been able to unite his northern Greek dominions to those in the Morea in the south, which were nominally under his suzerainty. But here the French principality had lapsed into anarchy and the initiative lay with the Byzantines. They had never lost a foothold in the south of the peninsula and this they were now able to enlarge into a province under an imperial governor. As the reconquest of lost territory in the Morea proceeded, the pro-Byzantine faction in Epiros gained ground. The independent rulers of Thessaly were less ready to bury the past. But by the early fourteenth century there was a hope that at least a part of northern Greece might some day be reincorporated into the empire.

If this hope were to be fulfilled, a watchful eye would have to be kept on the rapidly expanding Kingdom of Serbia, which had openly sided with Charles of Anjou against Byzantium. Michael VIII had failed to bring its rulers to heel and in the last years of his reign they had pushed their frontiers south into Greek Macedonia. In 1282 King Stephen Milutin captured Skopia (Skoplje). The approaches to Thessalonica were under threat. The Byzantine emperor could not hope to meet the challenge by force. He therefore offered his sister Eudokia in marriage to the Serbian king. Milutin was delighted, but Eudokia flatly refused to forsake the comforts of Constantinople for the rustic simplicity of the Serbian court. In desperation the emperor offered his own daughter Simonis in her place, though she was only five years old. It was a scandalous proposal which horrified the patriarch. But the wedding took place in 1299 and Milutin was content, since his bride's dowry included all the Byzantine territory which he had already conquered. For twenty years thereafter there was peace between Byzantium and Serbia, and the Serbian court and administration came more and more under the civilizing influence of Byzantine culture.

## The collapse of the eastern frontiers

For the European provinces of the empire, fragmented though they still were, there was some promise of recovery at the end of the thirteenth century. But in Asia Minor there was none. By 1300 only a few isolated cities held out against the new Turkish invaders. Andronikos II was no stranger to the eastern frontiers. From 1290 to 1293 he took personal command in the vital province of Bithynia, repairing the defences and recreating the frontier defence force. But in other districts the Byzantine resistance was hampered by local rebellions and mutinies, often inspired by the political enemies of the house of Palaiologos. In 1295 a Byzantine general, Alexios Philanthropenos, who had victoriously driven back the Turks in the Meander valley, was hailed as emperor. The revolt was soon suppressed but it was symptomatic of the feeling of the Greeks of Asia Minor that they had been too long abandoned and neglected by their government. Many weighed up their prospects and voluntarily went over to the Turks. Others, in ever increasing numbers, fled to the coast or to Constantinople to add to the crowds of homeless and destitute refugees.

In 1302 the emperor sent his son Michael to southern Asia Minor at the head of a great army. It included a contingent of Alans who had been driven out by the Mongols north of the Danube and taken into the imperial service as mercenaries. Yet more taxes had to be levied to equip and mount them. The Alans proved to be hopelessly unreliable. One company deserted, leaving their imperial commander stranded. Another fought and lost a battle dangerously near home in Bithynia in July 1302. The Turks were there led by a *ghazi* chieftain called Osman. This was the first appearance on the Byzantine scene of the founder of the Osmanli or Ottoman people. He followed up his victory by ravaging the land around the cities of Nikomedia, Nicaea and Prousa. Yet more refugees swarmed across to Constantinople. In 1302 Osman was only one among a large number of such *ghazi* leaders carving out little principalities or emirates in western and southern Asia Minor. Better known to the Byzantines and to the Italians in the Greek islands, were the emirs of Aydin and of Menteshe to the north and south of the Meander river. They were the first of the new Turks to take to the sea and to raid the coastline and islands, among them Rhodes which the Knights of St. John took from them in 1308. The emir of Aydin was to capture Ephesos in 1304 and then Smyrna, and his pirate fleet spread terror through the islands and as far as the mainland of Greece. No one could then have foreseen that the comparatively obscure emirate of Osman in Bithynia, closest of all to Constantinople, would be the only one to have an enduring effect on the world's history.

## The Catalan Company

After the disasters of 1302 the emperor clutched at every straw, even negotiating with the Mongols of Persia to exert their authority over the Turks. To help finance the army which he now belatedly saw to be needed, he decreed that the church and the monasteries must give up some of their benefices. He must have known that the decree would never be obeyed. Then, out of the blue, came a new ray of hope. A band of professional mercenaries known as the Catalan Company offered him their services. They had been defending Sicily on behalf of the King of Aragon for some years. But in 1302 they were paid off and looking for new employment. Their price was prodigious. Their leader Roger de Flor demanded four months pay in advance at an inflated rate. But the emperor thanked heaven that some good could come out of the west, signed a contract and sealed it by giving Roger his niece in marriage and the title of

Grand Duke. In September 1303 the Catalan Company, some 6,500 strong, arrived at Constantinople. They were a restless lot, prone to rioting and looting. They had to be got out of the city and let loose in Asia Minor without delay. In 1304 they marched as far south as Philadelphia terrorizing Greeks and Turks alike. From there on they made their own plans.

Other mercenaries which the emperor had employed had been answerable to him through their Greek commanders. The Catalans, however, formed a private army who took orders only from their own leader. When, after a series of misunderstandings and mistakes, their leader was murdered, the Catalans went berserk. They massacred or enslaved all the inhabitants of the peninsula of Gallipoli and declared it to be Spanish soil. For more than two years they devastated the countryside of Thrace on the western doorstep of Constantinople, inviting Turkish warriors across to join them in their depredations. The emperor tried and failed to dislodge them. Only when they had made a desert of Thrace did they move west towards Thessalonica. They plundered the monasteries of Mount Athos, but the walls of Thessalonica held them off and they were diverted south into Thessaly and on to Athens. There they finally came to rest in 1311, having overwhelmed the French Duke of Athens in a pitched battle; and there they proudly set up the Spanish flag which they had planted at Gallipoli. The French Duchy of Athens and Thebes, which had been one of the by-products of the Fourth Crusade, passed for nearly 80 years under Catalan rule, until the Catalans in their turn were ousted by another band of mercenaries, the Navarrese Company, in 1388.

Roger de Flor had complained about the base metal of the coinage paid him by the emperor. Yet it was his exorbitant demands which had necessitated a further devaluation of the Byzantine currency. The imperial family had been forced to convert their gold and silver plate into coin to satisfy his troops. Still more drastic measures were taken to milk revenue from the rich landowners of Byzantium, to close their loopholes and curb their exemptions. Somehow the money was found. But the damage done by the Catalans and their Turkish accomplices could not be made good by money alone. When the Catalans moved on, the Turks stayed. Some took service with Milutin of Serbia, but about 2,000 dug themselves in at Gallipoli. They were not expelled until 1312. Agriculture in the fields west of Constantinople was impossible. Some of the land had been deliberately laid waste on the emperor's orders. The city itself was now packed with refugees from Thrace as well as from Asia Minor. A distressing picture of life in Constantinople in these years is given in the letters of the Patriarch Athanasios. Food was scarce and expensive. There was a flourishing black market in wheat.

Some merchants were actually exporting it to get higher prices elsewhere. Athanasios, a rigorous ascetic and stern moralist, earned the thanks of the poor and hungry by setting up soup kitchens for them and by badgering the emperor to appoint an official to supervise the sale of food and the baking of bread in the city. The import of wheat depended very largely on the Genoese, who loaded it at the ports of the Black Sea. But here too there were new problems. The Bulgarians, re-emerging from their long subjection to the Mongols, claimed the Black Sea ports as their own; and in 1307 the Emperor Andronikos tamely signed a treaty acknowledging the fact.

The emperor indeed had little initiative left. His policy wavered from one expedient to another. He tried to restore the fleet which he had earlier disbanded and to pay for a standing army. He still had hopes that the Ilkhan of the Mongols would send an army from the further east to rescue Asia Minor from the Turks. Such an army is said to have been sent to Bithynia in 1307. But it did little good. What Andronikos still dared not do was to invite the help of western Christendom against the infidel. Three of his subjects, however, were more adventurous or more desperate, one of them the then governor of Thessalonica. About 1307 they wrote to Charles of Valois, brother of Philip IV of France, and his wife Catherine of Courtenay, titular Latin Empress of Constantinople, proposing that Charles should lead an army to Byzantium to drive back the Turks. Nothing came of it and indeed it was a forlorn hope. Charles of Valois had, it was true, secured the pope's approval for a crusade to Constantinople and he had the support of Venice. But the same pope anathematized Andronikos II, and the purpose of the crusade was no other than the re-establishment of the Latin Empire. When the plan fell through in 1310, the Venetians prudently renewed their trade agreement with Byzantium. The Latin title to Constantinople soon passed to Charles's daughter, Catherine of Valois, who had become the second wife of Philip of Taranto. It was through them that the ghost of a claim to Constantinople continued to haunt some western minds. But in practice the Byzantines had little to fear from that ghost. The tragedy was that Greeks and Latins could never bring themselves to co-operate against the common enemy of their Christian faith.

## Church and emperor: the Patriarch Athanasios I

It was indeed that faith that kept them apart. Andronikos II was the most pious of Orthodox emperors, determined to live down the memory of his father's misdeeds. The Patriarch Athanasios, though unpopular even among the clergy for his puritanism and calls to duty, played on his emperor's piety. Andronikos was more at home with the problems of the church than with those of the empire, though like all true Byzantines he believed that the two were interdependent. He was particularly gratified to preside, in 1310, over the reconciliation of the Arsenites, those clergy and monks who still revered the memory of the long-dead patriarch who had excommunicated his father. It not only healed a rift in the church. It was also a belated acknowledgement of the legitimacy of the dynasty of Palaiologos. Andronikos also drew up a revised list of the bishoprics of the church and decreed that the monasteries of Mount Athos, which had come to have a new importance with the loss of so many monastic houses in Asia Minor, should henceforth be detached from imperial control and be placed under the sole authority of the patriarch of Constantinople. It was remarked even by contemporaries that the church under Andronikos II and the Patriarch Athanasios grew in stature and authority as the empire declined. A cartoon of the day showed the patriarch leading his emperor along like a donkey. But it is a fact that Athanasios, encouraged by his emperor, reaffirmed the prestige of the see of Constantinople as the head of all the Orthodox communities both in and beyond the empire's boundaries; and he helped to sow the seeds of the spiritual revival in Byzantium which was to blossom so paradoxically throughout the Orthodox world in the middle of the fourteenth century.

Athanasios, a hermit by inclination, made himself so disliked by his calls to repentance that he was forced to resign in 1293. Ten years later he was recalled from his cell in a wave of popular frenzy as the only prophet and messenger of God who could save his people. But in 1309 he finally gave up the struggle to cure them of their sins and retired for ever. It has been said that his only fault was to look upon the whole empire as a monastery. His letters to the emperor and other officials are full of denunciations of the prevailing corruption and depravity of the Byzantines, the avarice of the clergy, the worldliness of the monks and the delinquency of bishops lounging about in the capital when they should have been guarding or dying with their flocks in Asia Minor. He exaggerates but he speaks the truth. Corruption there was. Offices in the administration could be bought by the rich. Bribery could win influence in the right places. Tax collection was a fruitful enterprise for the collectors. And the worldly wealth of the great monasteries was well known. These sins were not new in Byzantine society but they had become more obvious as that society became smaller and more ingrown with the territorial shrinkage of the empire. The glaring disparity between the wealthy landowners of the ruling class and the abject poor of the town and countryside also became more apparent. The circumstances might have made for revolution or for a reform and restructuring of society. But the Byzantines were not given to the idea of reformation. They believed that the order of society was ordained by God. The poor, like the rich, were elements of that order. The best that could be done was to change or reform the leadership of society.

## The first civil war

Revolution in this form began in 1321. By then Andronikos II had been on the throne for nearly 40 years. He had made careful plans for securing the succession through his son Michael IX and his grandson Andronikos III. But these too, like so many of his other plans, had collapsed. Michael died in 1320. His son Andronikos III, who had been crowned as co-emperor in 1316, had developed into a dissolute youth. One of his amorous adventures resulted in the accidental death of his own brother, a disaster which is said to have hastened his father's death. The old emperor Andronikos, who had once held his grandson as his favourite, now disinherited him. These were the events that precipitated the first of the civil or dynastic wars that were to cripple the empire in the fourteenth century. The Byzantine historians of the time, who were directly involved in these events, describe them in terms of personalities. The causes clearly lay deeper. But the strict rules of Byzantine historiography and rhetoric forbade discussion of anything so sordid as social or economic factors.

When Andronikos III was disinherited in 1321 his cause was immediately taken up by a circle of his friends who persuaded him to fight for his right to the succession. They were mostly of an age with himself, members of the younger generation of the hereditary aristocracy. Foremost among them were John Cantacuzene, Theodore Synadenos and Syrgiannes Palaiologos. Cantacuzene came of a well-connected family who owned vast estates in Macedonia, northern Thrace and Thessaly, districts which had so far escaped any worse horrors than increased taxation and loss of their immunities. His career as a soldier and statesman, which began effectively with the first civil war, was to lead him eventually to the throne. Much of Byzantine history in the fourteenth century was to be determined by his policies and to be narrated by his pen in the memoirs which he composed in later life. Theodore Synadenos also belonged to the landed aristocracy and held a military command in Thrace. Syrgiannes, though of foreign extraction, was no parvenu, being related to the Palaiologi as well as the Cantacuzene family. A fourth accomplice was a man of comparatively obscure origins,

Alexios Apokaukos, whom Cantacuzene, the patron of his fortunes, depicts as an ungrateful and unscrupulous adventurer.

The ground for rebellion was prepared in northern Thrace. At Easter 1321 the young Andronikos III escaped from Constantinople and joined his friends at Adrianople. There he was hailed as emperor and assured himself of the people's loyalty by announcing an end to taxation. The economic measures of Andronikos II had bitten hard on the gentry of Thrace and they were eager to finance an army for his overthrow. The struggle was fought out in three stages. The old emperor had his own loyal supporters and he had the advantage of being in possession of Constantinople. He suggested compromises which proved unacceptable or unworkable. For a few years he conceded that his grandson might reign jointly with him in Constantinople; and Andronikos III was formally crowned as his colleague in 1325. It was probably at this stage that the double-headed eagle first became the device of the house of Palaiologos, symbolizing not, as is often thought, a great empire that looked at once to east and west, but a sordid division of imperial authority between two disputatious emperors of the same family. The future history of that family was to show how apt a device it was.

But half an empire was not enough for the partisans of the young Andronikos and in 1327 the final round of the conflict began. This time it was on a larger scale, since the kingdoms of Serbia and Bulgaria intervened on opposite sides. In January 1328 Thessalonica declared for Andronikos III; and in May of the same year, accompanied by his friend John Cantacuzene, he forced his way into Constantinople. Andronikos II was now at last persuaded to abdicate. He died as a monk four years later. His friend and counsellor, the Grand Logothete and scholar Theodore Metochites, who had been faithful to the end, was sent into exile. He was soon allowed to return, and he too died as a monk in 1332 in the beautiful monastery of the Chora, on whose repair and decoration he had lavished his riches. It was like the passing of an age. Andronikos II was 73 and had reigned for nearly half a century. A new generation with new ideas was now to take over.

# 3

# A kingdom divided

## The loss of Asia Minor to the Turks

The years of uncertainty and warfare between 1321 and 1328 had paralysed the administration, ruined the economy, disrupted agriculture and weakened still further the empire's resistance to its enemies. The Serbians, the Bulgarians, the Italians, and above all the Turks had all seen ways of profiting from the confusion. Turkish pirates had raided the coast of Thrace. But in Asia Minor the Osmanlis had been given a free hand to expand their emirate. In April 1326 they captured the city of Prousa. The end of Byzantine rule in Bithynia was in sight. Prousa (Bursa) became the first capital of the Osmanli state and there Osman was buried when he died in that same year, leaving his son Orchan to continue the holy war against the Christians. The new Byzantine government, young and vigorous though its leaders were, faced fearsome tasks. Andronikos III wore the crown but the effective ruler and formulator of policy was John Cantacuzene. He was a soldier by training and he was content with the office of Grand Domestic or commander-in-chief of the armies. Of their accomplices, Syrgiannes was rewarded with the governorship of Thessalonica, Synadenos was made Prefect of Constantinople, and Apokaukos was appointed controller of the treasury.

Even under its new management Byzantium could not find the strength to drive the Osmanlis out of Bithynia. The fact was proved in 1329 when Cantacuzene and his emperor took an army across the water. In June they were routed by Orchan and his warriors in two battles near Nikomedia. This was the first direct military encounter between a Byzantine emperor and an Osmanli emir. It would be futile to attempt a second. In 1331 the city of Nicaea fell to Orchan. Nikomedia was to fall in 1337. The Byzantines were never ashamed to bargain with their enemies. Diplomacy was often less humiliating than war. In August 1333 Andronikos III invited Orchan to meet him in Bithynia. A treaty was signed, the first between Greeks and Turks, and the emperor agreed to pay an annual tribute. The decision to come to terms was surely made by John Cantacuzene. Soldier though he was, he saw no future in looking for a military solution to the problem in Asia Minor. It was too late. The Greek inhabitants had lost heart. Thousands of them had already gone over to the Turks and even become Muslims. The rate of Christian apostasy to Islam appalled the leaders of the church. The people of Nicaea, seat of the first Council of the Church and former capital of the Christian Empire, made their own terms with their Muslim conquerors; and within ten years many of them had forsaken their Christianity. The patriarch of Constantinople vainly addressed anguished appeals to them. But the success of the Osmanlis was partly due to their own tolerance. Christians who did not resist their conquest were protected and encouraged to see the material advantages of joining the Muslim fold, where they were welcomed as fellow Osmanlis. There was little sense of ethnic exclusiveness in the primitive Ottoman state. The Christian church in Asia Minor went under remarkably quickly and easily.

The same policy of diplomatic recognition was soon adopted towards some of the other Turkish emirates further south. In the autumn of 1329 the emperor seized the chance offered by a local rebellion to take back the island of Chios from the Genoese. Chios lies off the coast from Smyrna, the district occupied by the emir of Aydin, whose pirate ships caused such havoc in the islands that a 'league of Christian powers' had been formed to deal with him. The league, sponsored by the pope, was mainly supported by the Knights of Rhodes and the French kings of Cyprus, and the Christian powers did not regard the Byzantines as being full members. Once again, much could have been achieved by co-operation between Christians. But the general effect of the league's activities, which did not stop short of seizing Byzantine territory, was to drive the Byzantines into closer alliance with the Turks. In 1335, when the Genoese helped by the Knights occupied Lesbos, Andronikos III called on the emir of Aydin to lend him ships to recover the island. The treaty then signed implicitly recognized the independent existence of yet another Muslim emirate; and Umur, the ruler of Aydin, struck up a personal friendship with John Cantacuzene which was to secure him a ready supply of troops and ships in the future. These were dangerous tactics perhaps. The westerners thought them to be further proof of Byzantine deviousness and treachery. But they secured peace on that front for several years. It was better to have the Turks as allies than as enemies. They seemed to be rather more reliable than the Italians.

## The recovery of northern Greece

Andronikos III was more energetic than his grandfather. He was also more fortunate in the opportunities that presented themselves to him. The idea of reuniting to the empire the lost provinces in northern Greece, on which Andronikos II had worked, became a reality during his grandson's reign. In Thessaly the last descendant of the separatist Greek dynasty had died in 1318. For some years there was anarchy. Albanian nomads began to descend into the plains. The Catalans moved in from Thebes in the south. Only a few local lords kept order in their own domains. In 1333, when the most successful of them died, the emperor, who was then in Macedonia, saw the chance to send in an army and reclaim Thessaly as a Byzantine province. The inhabitants came to terms and an imperial governor was appointed. The reincorporation of Epiros came a few years later. Here there was a strong faction in favour of direct rule from Constantinople. Its opponents, however, had a willing ally across the water in Italy where Catherine of Valois saw a way to press her ghostly claim to the Latin Empire of Constantinople. She sent a fleet to Epiros to foment a revolt on behalf of the young heir to the title of independent Despot of Epiros. But in 1340 Andronikos III and his Grand Domestic John Cantacuzene arrived on the scene with an army. Cantacuzene persuaded the inhabitants of the benefits of Byzantine rule. The revolt was crushed. The Italian fleet melted away; and the last Despot of Epiros was taken off to Constantinople. An imperial governor was appointed to administer the province of Epiros, which had been detached from the empire since 1204.

Contemporaries understandably hailed the restoration of the long-lost provinces of northern Greece as the greatest achievement of Andronikos III. It looked as if the emperor had been right to cut his losses in Asia Minor and to concentrate on the revival of Byzantium as a great power in Europe. But the revival was an illusion. Only a few years later the whole of northern Greece except for Thessalonica was to pass into the Kingdom of Serbia. In 1330 the Serbians had won a crushing victory over their neighbours in Bulgaria at Velbužd (Küstendil). The victory brought to the fore the greatest of all the medieval Serbian kings, Stephen Dušan. Like his predecessors Dušan had designs on Thessalonica. But his sights were ultimately set on the greater prize of Constantinople, on the title of emperor, and on the creation of a new form of universal empire in which Slavs would predominate over Greeks. In 1340, however, when Byzantine authority seemed so successfully re-established on the southern borders of his kingdom, Dušan was still nominally at peace with the Greeks.

## Domestic changes and reforms

The Byzantine Empire under Andronikos III certainly regained some of its lost prestige. Its enemies, actual and potential, had been shown that it still had some powers of resistance and recovery. Foreign policy on the grand scale of Michael VIII was out of the question. But Andronikos made some tentative efforts to interest the western world in his cause. In 1339 he broke a long silence by sending an emissary, in secret, to the pope at Avignon to suggest how discussions about the union of the churches might be resumed and co-operation between Christians be achieved. The pope was not impressed. Andronikos also made great efforts to maintain the army and navy and to strengthen the economy. His policy required huge sums of money to pay tribute to the Turks and wages to mercenary troops. But he had the solid backing of millionaires like John Cantacuzene who were willing to put their private fortunes behind a government in which they had confidence. It was also a government committed to stamping out the corruption of which the Patriarch Athanasios had complained. The rule of law, the universal Roman law of the empire, must prevail. Local landlords and magnates must no longer be allowed to interpret it for themselves. Andronikos II had tried and failed to set up a high court of appeal. His grandson created four supreme and universal justices with exceptional powers to enforce the law throughout the empire. When bribery and corruption had become universal, however, it was hard to impose universal laws. The judges themselves were soon found to be corruptible. They were brought before the emperor and dismissed. But others took their place. Courts with similar powers were set up in other cities and provinces; and the institution of the supreme and universal justices lasted to the end of the empire. In the chaotic circumstances of the time many people preferred to take their cases before a church court where they felt more sure of impartiality. The church here also gained in authority at the expense of the empire. But it was in or just after the time of Andronikos III that the two last academic lawyers of Byzantium, Matthew Blastares and Constantine Harmenopoulos, made their compendia of law which were to be widely used and translated in the Slav as well as the Greek world long after the fall of Byzantium.

Universal law might be proposed but the universal empire was no more than a theory. It was a thing of shreds and patches. Andronikos II's Italian wife had suggested to him that her sons could be accommodated by the gift of royal appanages in the western style to which she was accustomed. The old emperor had refused to consider turning his monarchy into a polyarchy; and his wife had left him to live in Thessalonica and to find principalities for her sons in Italy and elsewhere. Things had changed since then. It had become accepted that the way to keep the shreds and patches together was to keep them in the family. The new governors in northern Greece were either relatives or close associates of Andronikos III and Cantacuzene. They governed by imperial favour rather than by decree the scattered cities and estates of a domain which the emperor and his family had come to regard as their private property. More and more the empire was becoming an aristocratic family concern bound together by intermarriage in the ruling class and by mutual self-preservation. It was soon to be shown that there was much opposition to this development.

## The second civil war

Next to the imperial house of Palaiologos the most powerful family was that of Cantacuzene. When Andronikos III died prematurely in June 1341, his eldest son John Palaiologos was only nine years old. It was widely assumed that his lifelong friend John Cantacuzene would step in as regent if not as emperor until the boy came of age. But Andronikos had made no explicit statement to this effect. Cantacuzene, who represented the wealth and influence of the landed aristocracy, was no favourite of the underprivileged town dwellers of Constantinople or Thessalonica. His rivals played on his unpopularity to accomplish his downfall. The widowed empress, Anne of Savoy, mother of John Palaiologos, had never liked him. She favoured the claim of the Patriarch John Kalekas to act as regent for her son. But the man who made the most out of the constitutional crisis was the upstart Alexios Apokaukos who owed his many lucrative appointments to John Cantacuzene. Apokaukos fed the fire of popular prejudice against his former patron and intrigued against him with the empress and the patriarch.

In September 1341 Cantacuzene left Constantinople to take an army to Greece. As soon as he was gone his rivals took over the city and ordered his surrender or arrest. The patriarch was proclaimed as regent; Apokaukos became Prefect of the City. Cantacuzene refused to submit. He made his headquarters, as he had done before, in northern Thrace where he could count on local loyalty. Those of his supporters in Constantinople who were not rounded up by his enemies joined him; and there in Thrace they proclaimed him as their emperor on 26 October 1341. He declined to take the crown, insisting that his proclamation had been forced upon him and that he was no more than the guardian of the legitimate heir John Palaiologos. From this principle he never deviated. But his rivals in Constantinople branded him as a usurper. The patriarch excommunicated him and in November crowned the boy emperor as John V.

A second civil war or struggle for power began. It was to last for nearly six years and to be even more destructive than the first. It gave much greater scope for intervention by foreign powers, especially the Serbians and the Turks; and it unleashed social and political forces which were normally inactive or suppressed in Byzantine society. When for a second time in a generation the people of Thrace and Macedonia saw that their land was about to become a battlefield for the ruling class, they rebelled. Their mood of rebellion was deliberately fostered by the regents in Constantinople, where Apokaukos incited the city mob to loot and destroy the property of Cantacuzene's family and friends. Soon after Cantacuzene's proclamation as emperor, the people of Adrianople rounded on their aristocracy and set up a revolutionary government. Other towns in Thrace followed their example. The movement originated in the urban centres and not in the countryside. It was no peasant revolt. And it is significant that the rebels everywhere declared their allegiance to the house of Palaiologos, to the young emperor John V and to the regency in Constantinople. They were not out to change the form of government, only to change its composition. They defined their objective in one word or slogan: it was the defeat of 'Cantacuzenism'.

## The Zealot revolution in Thessalonica

The movement had its most memorable and lasting effect in Thessalonica. There it was organized and managed by a faction who called themselves the Zealots. The spark of revolt was ignited when it became known that the aristocracy had called on John Cantacuzene to take over the city as emperor early in 1342. The imperial governor was thrown out; the houses of the rich were ransacked and burnt by the mob; and when the dust of rioting had settled the Zealots took control and set up a form of commune administration that was to last until 1350. Here as elsewhere the regency in Constantinople quickly recognized the new regime. Apokaukos appointed his son John as his deputy in Thessalonica, as he had earlier appointed his other son Manuel in Adrianople.

Thessalonica was the second biggest city in the Byzantine Empire, a crowded commercial centre with its international market and annual trade fair, and a busy port much frequented by Italians. It is tempting to see foreign influences at work behind the Zealot revolution, especially the influence of Genoa whose republic was going through similar revolutionary changes at about the same time. No such influence can be documented. It is tempting too to suggest that the Zealots held power by introducing a programme of social reform to alleviate the plight of the poor whose support they seem to have enjoyed. But there is little evidence to prove it. Almost all that is known about the Zealot regime derives from its victims or its opponents, principally John Cantacuzene himself and his older contemporary the historian Gregoras. Their accounts dwell on the horrors and massacres perpetrated by the revolutionaries. The terms which they employ are taken from classical Greek authors and not from the popular broadsheets of the time; and being aristocrats themselves they could only interpret the affair as a distressing and mercifully temporary aberration from the divinely ordained norm of order, the antithesis of confusion and revolt. The deeper significance of the revolution, if such existed, in social, economic, or political terms, therefore passed them by and remains a matter of speculation, some of it at great length, to this day.

John Cantacuzene remained imperturbably convinced of the justice of his own cause. Denied access to Thessalonica and cut off from his headquarters in Thrace, he sought refuge in Serbia. He was a man who made influential friends easily but trusted them perhaps too readily. Stephen Dušan of Serbia was an unfaithful ally who changed sides as it suited his own expansionist plans. Cantacuzene also called on the support of his friend Umur of Aydin, who twice sent Turkish troops to his rescue. With their help he was able to fight his way back to Thrace and then to concentrate on overcoming his rivals in Constantinople. Macedonia was thus left to its fate, and in September 1345 the Serbians captured the key city of Serres to the east of Thessalonica. In April 1346 Dušan was crowned with the title of Emperor of the Serbs and Greeks. There were now three claimants to the imperial title and the Serbian dream of a Slavo-Byzantine empire was a step nearer to fulfilment.

The regency in Constantinople, supported by the revolution any governments in the provincial towns, held the whip hand in the struggle for four years. The Empress Anne looked for support to Bulgaria as well as to Serbia, to the Venetians, the Genoese and the Turks, and even tried to interest the pope in her cause. But none of these potential allies had disinterested motives. Her funds were low and her army depleted. In 1343 she raised some money by pawning the crown jewels to Venice. They were never redeemed. Early in 1345 Adrianople surrendered to Cantacuzene and soon he was master of most of Thrace, or what was left of it, for his Turkish allies helped themselves to their own rewards and the country was once more reduced to a desert. The tide then turned in Cantacuzene's favour. Alexios Apokaukos, fearing a reaction in Constantinople, became more and more heavy-handed, until in June 1345 he was murdered by some of his political prisoners. Apokaukos had been a prime mover of the civil war. His murder brought the end of that war in sight. His son John at once led a counter-revolution in Thessalonica, offering to make over the city to Cantacuzene. But the time was not ripe. John lost his life in a welter of bloodshed through which the Zealots gained an even firmer hold on the city.

Latterly Cantacuzene lost the help of his Turkish friend Umur of Aydin. For in October 1344 the western league of Christian powers, reorganized by Pope Clement VI, had captured the port of Smyrna. Umur had his hands full defending his own patch and was indeed to die trying to recover Smyrna in 1348. But Cantacuzene had by then found another Turkish ally in the person of Orchan of Bithynia, which was nearer to the scene of action. In 1346 he gave his daughter Theodora in marriage to Orchan, who was glad to supply warriors to fight in Thrace. Cantacuzene has been much maligned for his reliance on the help of the Turks. He himself thought it necessary to apologize for setting Muslims to fight Christians. But he was not alone in seeking their support. The regency too employed them as mercenaries. The difference was that Cantacuzene naively hoped that by forging personal friendships with their emirs he could create understanding. But neither he nor they could control the barbarity of their soldiers when they were let loose on Christian soil.

## The end of civil war

On 21 May 1346, the feast of St Constantine and St Helena, John Cantacuzene allowed himself to be crowned as emperor at Adrianople. The ceremony was performed by the Patriarch of Jerusalem, a recent refugee from Constantinople. His partisans hoped that he would then inaugurate a dynasty and so protect their interests by proclaiming his eldest son Matthew as heir apparent. But this he refused to do. He preferred still to pose as guardian of the rights of the house of Palaiologos. It was a shrewd decision. Events had clearly shown that popular opinion was on that side. Finally, on the night of 2 February 1347, Cantacuzene contrived to enter Constantinople with a small body of men. The way had been prepared by his friends and there was almost no resistance. The Empress Anne had made a conciliatory gesture at the eleventh hour by condoning the dismissal of the regent and Patriarch John Kalekas. But nearly a week passed before she gave in and agreed to negotiate. The terms of the settlement were that Cantacuzene was to reign as senior colleague with the young emperor John Palaiologos for ten years; and the two families would be united by John's marriage to Cantacuzene's daughter Helena. There were to be no reprisals; all political prisoners would be released; the past was to be forgotten.

People at the time marvelled at the clemency of the victor to his former enemies. The revolutionary fervour of six years before had spent its force, much of it extinguished by the savage behaviour in Thrace of Cantacuzene's Turkish allies. Thessalonica was still under its own management, though the Zealot regime had degenerated into a selfish dictatorship, some of whose henchmen were planning to hold on to their power by inviting the Serbians into the city. But elsewhere there was a general and sincere sense of relief that the fighting was over. There had been many struggles for power and civil wars before in the long history of Byzantium, but never one in which the shortcomings of the social order had been so exposed. Society seemed exhausted by the effort and relieved to conceal the exposure so that the old order could be restored. There had been another dimension to the conflict, however, and one which was dearer to the Byzantine mind than mere politics.

## The hesychast controversy

In the last years of Andronikos III's reign the Byzantine church had been split by a new controversy. A small but influential group of monks, mainly on Mount Athos, were perfecting a technique of prayer and meditation which, they claimed, enabled them to see the divine light with mortal eyes, or to become illumined by the aura of the Transfiguration. They were to be known as the hesychasts. The name had for long been applied to solitary monks, as men who live alone in peace with God. Meditation in the Byzantine monastic tradition was not thought of as an end in itself. The goal of the perfect monk was no less than a vision of the divine light through which he might attain union, however momentary, with God and become himself deified. Deification or *theosis* was always supposed to be within the reach of the pure in heart. The writings of Byzantine mystics are full of metaphysical and theological ideas which the Latin church suspected as being misguided or dangerous. But the hesychasts in the fourteenth century were not breaking new ground. They were developing the practices and the theology of a long and unbroken tradition of Orthodox mysticism. Their technique of prayer, however, which involved bodily as well as mental discipline, laid them open to the ridicule of sceptics. They were denounced as charlatans by an Italian Greek called Barlaam of Calabria, a scholar monk who had been enjoying some fame as a visiting professor in Constantinople. Barlaam derided their methods and challenged their theology. Many Byzantines resented this incursion of an outsider into the field of Orthodox truth. But the man who fully rose to the challenge was Gregory Palamas, himself a monk and the main formulator of hesychast doctrine. Palamas was supported by his fellow monks on Athos but also by John Cantacuzene who, though he admired Barlaam's erudition, believed the theology of the hesychasts to be perfectly Orthodox. The patriarch was persuaded to convene a council of bishops to examine the case in June 1341. Barlaam was condemned and left for Italy.

The verdict in favour of the hesychasts was not, however, unanimous. Some Byzantine theologians and philosophers had their doubts. Notable among them were Gregory Akindynos, a friend of Palamas, and the scholar and historian Nikephoros Gregoras. In August 1341 a second council was held at which Akindynos was condemned and Palamas again vindicated. It was chaired by John Cantacuzene, for by then Andronikos III was dead and there was no emperor to preside. This circumstance helped to drag the debate down from the sublime heights of mystical theology into the mud of the political rivalry between Cantacuzene and the Patriarch John. The patriarch was no great theologian but he could make political capital out of the matter by painting Palamas as the protégé and partisan of Cantacuzene; and in this he was eagerly assisted by Gregory Akindynos and other anti-hesychasts. Palamas was arrested in Constantinople and then excommunicated. It is by no means certain that all those who sided with the regency in the second civil war were of like mind on the theological controversy. Opinions were divided even in the opposing political camps. But there can be no doubt that Cantacuzene, as the known champion of Palamas, derived invaluable benefit from having behind him the religious authority of the monks of Athos. His political victory in 1347 inevitably entailed the spiritual victory of Hesychasm. The controversy was not resolved in that year. But the Patriarch John was deposed and denounced, and his place was taken by a hesychast monk who had suffered for his convictions. It was he who performed the second coronation of Cantacuzene on 21 May 1347. Palamas was appointed to the See of Thessalonica.

## The reign of John VI Cantacuzene

The second coronation ceremony set the seal on John Cantacuzene's title as emperor in Constantinople. The marriage of his daughter to John V symbolized the end of conflict and the new harmony between the two ruling families. They were grand occasions. But neither could be held in St Sophia because there was no money to repair the damage done to the building by an earthquake in the previous year; and it was sadly observed that the crown jewels were made of glass and the plate at the wedding feast of pewter and clay. The real crown jewels were still in pawn to Venice and the gold and silver plate had long ago been melted down. The empire was indeed in poverty. Nor was it as united as might be made to appear. Cantacuzene still held by his intention to protect the rights of John V. Officials had to swear allegiance to both emperors. The arrangement was resented not only by the loyal supporters of the house of Palaiologos, who looked on Cantacuzene as a usurper and a hypocrite, but also by his own son Matthew, who had hoped to take precedence over John V. There was a danger that the civil war might be perpetuated by the rising generation.

John Cantacuzene, known in the history books as John VI, had many plans for the recovery of Byzantium. Some of them were promising. A few almost succeeded. But more and more the empire was at the mercy of its foreign enemies and competitors, who found it all too easy to profit from its difficulties and to exploit the latent rivalry between the two imperial families. This was one of the obstacles which John VI tried and failed to overcome. There were many others. In the very year of his victory Constantinople and other cities of the empire were afflicted by the Black Death, carried from the Crimea on Genoese ships. There are no reliable statistics of the number of its victims. They were perhaps innumerable. But the effect of the plague, which rapidly spread to western Europe, was to lower still further the morale and confidence of the Byzantines. Cantacuzene lost his youngest son. But a more eminent victim in his family was the cousin whom he had appointed to govern Thessaly and Epiros. Northern Greece, so recently restored to the empire, was left leaderless. Stephen Dušan saw his chance and in 1348 two Serbian armies marched in. Within a few months both Greek provinces had been added to his Serbian empire which now extended from the Danube and the Adriatic Sea to the Gulf of Corinth. If he could include the city of Thessalonica in his conquests, Dušan would be master of an empire vastly superior in size and strength to the remnants of Byzantium. In the event, however, he was forestalled and the Zealot faction who were plotting the surrender of Thessalonica to him were outwitted. In 1350 Cantacuzene, backed by a fleet and a huge army sent by his Turkish son-in-law Orchan, entered the city. Most of the citizens welcomed him and the last of the revolutionary leaders were arrested and deported.

Thessalonica, now restored to the empire after eight years of autonomy, was declared to be the capital of the junior Emperor John V. Cantacuzene developed still further the principle of family government. His eldest son Matthew had been granted an appanage in Thrace. In 1349 he sent his second son Manuel to take charge of the province in the Morea with the rank of Despot. Now that Asia Minor was almost wholly lost to the Turks and northern Greece to the Serbians, Thrace and the Morea were the two most important fragments of empire. It was as well to keep them in the family; and certainly Manuel's administration in the Morea was soon to bring a new lease of life to Byzantine Greece. But Cantacuzene's appointment of his son-in-law John to Thessalonica was not so inspired; and if he thought that he could foster a family relationship with the Osmanlis through his other son-in-law Orchan he was soon to be deceived. There were bands of marauding Turks already roaming the plains and coast of Thrace. They only lacked a leader to weld them into a force for the conquest of the whole of eastern Europe.

## Byzantium at the mercy of Genoa and Venice

High on Cantacuzene's list of plans for recovery was the rebuilding of a strong fleet of warships for defence and of merchant ships for economic independence. The former might help to deter Stephen Dušan, who was vainly trying to interest the Venetians in lending him ships for an attack on Constantinople. The latter might help to break the hold of the Genoese on Byzantine trade. The Genoese had helped to finance the regency during the civil war. In 1346 they had again seized control of Chios. The annual revenue of their colony at Galata was reckoned to be nearly seven times that of Constantinople itself, and they had plans for extending its area and its fortifications. If the mood took them they could reduce the Byzantines to bankruptcy and starvation. To divert merchant traffic from Galata to his own harbours, the emperor lowered the tariffs payable by ships unloading at Constantinople. He then set about raising funds for the construction of a new fleet. The Genoese began to see that their lucrative monopoly might be broken. In 1348, while the emperor was away, they sailed over and attacked the Byzantine shipyards. The Byzantines were now inflamed to action. New taxes were levied and money was more willingly provided for revenge; and in the spring of 1349 the revived Byzantine navy put to sea to humiliate the Genoese. It was destroyed in its first battle. Nevertheless, the Genoese had been impressed. They agreed to recognize Cantacuzene as emperor and even to pay rent for the possession of Chios. They must have known that the Venetians had already recognized the new regime. Venice, always eager to be in on any conflict with Genoa, renewed its treaty with the emperor in September 1349. Cantacuzene may have hoped that he was thus assured of protection against both Italian republics. But in fact it was they who were embroiling him in their own quarrel, which came to blows again in August 1350. Once more the emperor was forced into taking sides in a dispute which was none of his making and which was fought in Byzantine waters over the control of Byzantine trade. The climax came in February 1352 with a great sea battle in the Bosporos. Byzantine ships fought alongside a fleet sent out from Venice. The outcome was inconclusive and the Venetians sailed off leaving the emperor to make what terms he could with the Genoese at Galata.

More and more the survival of Byzantium depended on the mercy of its enemies and exploiters. Cantacuzene laboured to secure economic freedom from the Italians and to protect the home market by reducing customs dues and levying new forms of taxation. He was doomed to fail. The Italians soon learnt that what they could not achieve by warfare among themselves they could accomplish by provoking the rivalry among the Byzantine ruling families. In Thessalonica, where John V had been installed as emperor, there was a clique urging him to renounce his agreement with his father-in-law. The Venetians offered to subsidize his rebellion. The Serbians too were keen to support him. For a time Cantacuzene managed to keep the peace by transferring John to an appanage in Thrace. His place in Thessalonica was taken by his mother, Anne of Savoy, who thereafter reigned as empress over her own portion of empire until her death in 1365. But in 1352 open war broke out in Thrace between John V and Matthew Cantacuzene, the former encouraged by Serbia and Venice, the latter by Turkish troops supplied by Orchan. The battles for the Byzantine throne were now being waged almost independently of the protagonists by their Serbian and Turkish allies, the Italians acting as brokers. The Turks proved to be more ruthless and effective. In 1353 John V was captured and deported to the small island of Tenedos near the mouth of the Hellespont. Matthew Cantacuzene was proclaimed and then crowned as co-emperor with his father. The dynasty of Cantacuzene seemed at last to be replacing that of Palaiologos.

## The abdication of John Cantacuzene

But public opinion was against the change. The patriarch refused to perform the coronation of Matthew and resigned. A new patriarch had to be created for the ceremony. Cantacuzene's popularity had not grown with the years. His efforts seemed to have put Byzantium more than ever at the mercy of its enemies; and in particular his constant reliance on military support from the Turks had greatly damaged his cause. His personal and family relationship with Orchan had proved useful, but it could not last for ever. Orchan's son Suleiman did not allow it to hamper his own movements. In 1352 Suleiman's troops had occupied a fortress near Gallipoli. It was the first permanent settlement of the Osmanlis on European soil. Two years later, in March 1354, Gallipoli itself was destroyed by an earthquake and Suleiman moved in to occupy the ruins and rebuild the city. Gallipoli, which the Catalans had once found so useful, was the key point controlling the passage across the Hellespont from Asia to Europe. Not even Orchan felt like relinquishing it, and Turkish settlers were soon making their way over in large numbers.

The reaction against Cantacuzene now came to a head. In November 1354 John V sailed from Tenedos and slipped into Constantinople by night. The people greeted him with enthusiasm. In December, after a brief attempt at joint rule, Cantacuzene abdicated and entered a monastery. It was as the monk Joasaph and not as the Emperor John VI that he wrote his memoirs and his theological works, some in defence of Hesychasm whose political champion he had been, some in defence of Christianity against the Muslims to whom he had sacrificed his daughter and, some would say, had sold his empire. But he had made too great a mark on Byzantine affairs to be left as a recluse. His monastery was not in the wilderness but in the heart of Constantinople; and his influence, whether directly or as a grey eminence behind the throne, was to be felt for many years to come. His family too remained influential. His son Manuel still held office as Despot in the Morea. His elder son Matthew, who had been given the crown and title of emperor, refused at first to abandon either. For more than two years there was fighting in Thrace between John V and Matthew, between the families of Palaiologos and Cantacuzene, until Matthew was defeated by a Serbian army and handed over to his rival. He was sent to join his brother in the Morea and for a short while took over there when Manuel died in 1380. It was there too, at Mistra, which the Cantacuzene brothers had transformed into the most prosperous and enlightened provincial city left in the empire, that their father, the emperor-monk John-Joasaph, went to spend the declining years of his long and varied life. He died in June 1383.

# 4

# Cultural and spiritual revival

## Patronage and education

The monastery church of the Chora, the Kariye Djami, in Constantinople, now so carefully and lovingly restored, stands as an abiding monument to Byzantine taste and sophistication in the fourteenth century. Its mosaics and wall-paintings are eloquent of the living continuity of the Byzantine artistic tradition. Its very existence speaks of the undiminished vigour of Orthodox spirituality. It was once the centre of a vast complex of monastic buildings with a well-stocked library. The long and almost unbroken tradition of Byzantine education and scholarship also continued into the fourteenth century. The founder of this monastery in its final form was Theodore Metochites, Grand Logothete and friend of the Emperor Andronikos II, who died in 1332. He was one of the greatest scholars of the middle ages. Once again it is tempting to look for a common influence behind parallel developments in east and west at this time, to recall that the Chora monastery was being decorated just at the moment when Giotto was at work in Padua, that Gregory Palamas was the contemporary of Tauler and Eckhart, or that Metochites could have known William of Ockham. The parallels could be extended to infinity. There were no points of convergence. The two societies were quite literally worlds apart. Palamas knew nothing of Latin theology and cared less. Metochites knew not a word of Latin and prided himself on the exclusively 'Hellenic' foundations of his scholarship.

Art, scholarship and even the monastic life thrived on patronage. The emperor was the supreme patron and benefactor of all. But the great families, such as that of Metochites, played their part too. Many other churches and works of art bear the names of such wealthy patrons, in Thessalonica as well as in the capital. The monastery of the Virgin Pammakaristos in Constantinople, for example, was founded about 1310 by the family of Glabas; the convent of the Virgin of Good Hope was endowed in the thirteenth century, and its charter, now in Oxford, lists and portrays the numerous descendants of the foundress and reveals the network of judicious marriages by which they sustained their wealth and her foundation. The Byzantine ruling class of this age may have bought, bribed or married their way to the top. But they took a pride in certain standards of culture, piety and erudition which they inherited from a more glorious age and which reached new heights of excellence in the otherwise desolate years of the early fourteenth century.

Literacy and education were never a clerical monopoly in Byzantium. The ancient Greco-Roman tradition of secular education had never been completely broken as it was in the west in the dark ages. Byzantium had its dark age in the seventh and eighth centuries but at the end of it education revived and flourished as though there had been little interruption. There had always been a well-educated laity. In the dark age after the Fourth Crusade, when the Byzantines had to pick up the pieces of their traditions in exile, education, scholarship, art and culture were not allowed to die out. They were vital elements of those traditions. Education had generally been directed towards equipping young men with the basic knowledge and the required polish for entry into the administration or the church. The basic knowledge was unhesitatingly derived from the literature of antiquity, through laborious and somewhat unimaginative learning, often by heart, of the ancient Greek authors and poets. As Metochites, who was far beyond the basic stage, was to remark: the ancient Hellenes said it all and there is nothing left for us to say. It is often flatteringly stated that every educated Byzantine could quote Homer and the classics, as if this were a mark of his impeccable erudition. In fact the teaching of the classics was often done through *florilegia* or anthologies of quotations, at the compilation of which schoolmasters were prolific. The Byzantines particularly enjoyed compiling facts and putting together lexicons and encyclopaedias. But the polish of education, which fitted a man to become a bureaucrat or a bishop, was rhetoric. Rhetoric was the canker in the cultural blood of the Byzantines. Of all the legacy of Greek antiquity available to them the rhetorical literature of the Second Sophistic was the part they most admired and the part that was most restricting to their intellectual honesty and freedom.

The other restraint on their intellectual liberty was the church, though religion and rhetoric went together. St Basil of Caesarea and St Gregory of Nyssa were read for their style as well as for their content. They themselves had studied at the rhetorical fount at Athens in their day. Few Byzantines, however, consciously felt that the freedom of their thought was trammelled by the bonds of their faith. They were aware that much of their Hellenic heritage from the ancient world was at variance with the revealed truths of Christianity and therefore dangerous and to be discarded. The word Hellene was regularly used to mean pagan. In the eleventh century one of their brightest philosophers, John Italos, pupil and successor of the celebrated Michael Psellos, had been outlawed by church and state for taking his Hellenic studies too far and so perverting his students as well as endangering his own soul. For many years thereafter the teaching of philosophy in Constantinople was committed to the safe keeping of the church. It seems likely that people preferred it that way.

After 1204 a fresh start had to be made in education as in everything else. There were learned men among the refugees who fled to Epiros and to Nicaea. Some of the bishops in Epiros were highly polished products of the Constantinopolitan school and one of them, Bardanes of Corfu, was renowned for the allegedly 'Attic' purity of his rhetorical style. But the institutions of education no longer existed and there was a shortage of books and libraries. It was in the Empire of Nicaea rather than in Epiros that these problems were faced. As the years went on the empire in exile needed new recruits for its civil service and its church. Most of the highest positions in court circles, many of which were purely honorary, were in the emperor's gift and filled from the aristocratic families. Those selected would receive their schooling at court and then proceed either to the civil service or to the army. There was still some social mobility. The last of the emperors at Nicaea in particular extended his patronage to men of quite humble origins. Candidates for the lower offices in the administration were educated at private schools, which existed in several cities in Asia Minor. The primary schooling consisted of the *hiera grammata*, the elements of literacy taught chiefly through Christian texts; the secondary education was known as the *enkyklios paideia* or curriculum of grammar, poetry, rhetoric and mathematics. Higher education was harder to come by, though latterly, again through imperial patronage, it was revived on a limited scale by the enterprise of a few individuals.

The most influential of these were Nikephoros Blemmydes and his pupil George Akropolites. Blemmydes, who was born seven years before the Fourth Crusade, lived through the years of exile and died eleven years after the restoration of the empire. He more than any other single scholar carried the torch of learning forward through two generations. His learning ranged over many fields, in medicine, physics, philosophy, logic, mathematics, astronomy and theology; and his thirst for knowledge led him to travel to Greece, Mount Athos and elsewhere in search of lost or scattered manuscripts. The emperor helped him to found a school in Nicaea, though he spent the last quarter century of his life teaching his chosen pupils at his own rather exclusive monastery at Ephesos.

Among his prize students at Nicaea were the Emperor Theodore II Laskaris, for whom he wrote a treatise on kingship, and the future historian and statesman George Akropolites. Akropolites was to be a key figure in the continuation of scholarship in the restored empire after 1261. He led the Byzantine delegation to the Council of Lyons in 1274 not, it seems, through any very strong commitment to the cause of union, but because he was an experienced diplomat and a faithful servant of his emperor. It was to him that Michael VIII entrusted the task of recreating an educational system in Constantinople. The fruits of his enthusiastic efforts were to be seen during the reign of Andronikos II, when intellectual life and scholarship blossomed almost more abundantly than ever before in Byzantium.

Whether or not the institution of higher education over which Akropolites and his successors presided can be dignified with the name of university is doubtful. The number of their students was never great. It has been estimated that there were no more than about 100 men of letters and scholars in Constantinople in the middle of the fourteenth century. Higher education was an elitist pursuit, and much of it was clearly imparted through an individual or tutorial relationship between scholar and pupil rather than on an institutional basis. The church, however, seems to have maintained an academy of sorts with its appointed professors. The church was sometimes guarded in its attitude to secular learning; but it seems seldom to have suspected that any of the philosophers of the thirteenth or fourteenth centuries were overstepping the line and in need of correction or discipline. Not until the very last days did a Byzantine scholar emerge who was to question the fundamental truths of Christian Orthodoxy.

## The rediscovery of the Hellenic heritage

Under the patronage of Andronikos II the revival of learning acquired an astonishing momentum. Contemporaries, always with an eye to their Hellenic roots, compared his court to the Lyceum or the stoa of ancient Athens. Their rhetorical training obliged them to express the affairs of their own day in classical terms. The upstart races of the middle ages, for example, whose names were unknown to Herodotus and Thucydides, had to be translated into their ancient equivalents for polite consumption. The Turks became the Persians, the Bulgarians the Mysians, and the Serbians the Triballi. The coterie of intellectuals who read their learned papers or their highly artificial correspondence to their admiring peers at the emperor's soirees almost believed that the war against the Turks, which they left mainly to foreign mercenaries, was a new chapter in the ancient struggle of Greeks against Persians. But out of the fog of unreality some true scholarship emerged. It took the form of rediscovery rather than renaissance, a rediscovery of many long-neglected or forgotten works of antiquity. A real renaissance of learning would have required some originality in the use of the material. But in this the latterday Byzantines were curiously deficient. They excelled in learned commentaries and paraphrases of the classics. They laboured to some purpose in the pedantic vineyard of textual emendation; and their scribes undoubtedly preserved for posterity many texts which would otherwise have been lost. Not without reason have the Byzantines been called the librarians of the middle ages. But they built surprisingly little on the ancient foundations which their diligence unearthed.

They were not a materialistic people and they had no mind for applied science or technology. Some advances were made in the art of medicine, partly as a result of Persian influence coming through from Trebizond. But there were no great innovations or inventions in agriculture, warfare or engineering. The pseudo-sciences of astrology, divination and magic, though repeatedly condemned by the church, continued to flourish in the cities as well as in the countryside. The magical books of antiquity were still being secretly copied and distributed in the fourteenth century and pagan festivals were still being held in the villages. Perhaps the most original contribution of the scholars of this age was in the field of the theoretical sciences, in mathematics and astronomy. George Akropolites taught both mathematics and philosophy. His pupil George Pachymeres, who was born at Nicaea and died at Constantinople about 1310, composed a Handbook of the Four Sciences or *Quadrivium* in which his own interest in mathematics and astronomy is evident. He also wrote philosophical and theological works besides the history of his age, for which he is best known. His contemporary Maximos Planoudes shared the revived interest in mathematics and introduced the use of the zero into the Greek numerical system. Both he and Pachymeres recommended the adoption of Arabic numerals to facilitate calculations, but they made few converts. Similarly, Nikephoros Gregoras gave a lecture at the imperial court on a possible reform of the Julian Calendar. But nothing came of it.

These scholars, however, would have disliked being labelled as specialists. Their aim was to encompass the whole field of human knowledge, as Blemmydes had tried to do. The two of his successors who came nearest to achieving this aim were Gregoras and his teacher Theodore Metochites. Both were men of the world, not cloistered monks or sheltered academics. Metochites had an active public career as Grand Logothete of Andronikos II. But he found time to read all the available philosophical and scientific works of Greek antiquity. The collection of his essays which has survived reveals the truly encyclopaedic quality of his erudition, derivative though it was. But again his chief joy was in mathematics and astronomy, to the study of which he came quite late in life. This too was derivative and not original; and it was narrowly Greek in scope, for Metochites would have nothing to do with what he called 'foreign' theories or systems. But he imparted his love for these subjects to his pupil Gregoras, who became a greater scholar than his master. Gregoras lived through and wrote the history of the two civil wars and of the theological controversy that disrupted his society in the fourteenth century. He was a philosopher of the platonist school and a theologian of rigidly conservative views. He took great delight in trouncing Barlaam of Calabria in public debate and in discountenancing some papal legates in Constantinople in the 1330s. He was a somewhat arrogant and tedious man. But in the study of astronomy he put his learning to some practical use. Apart from his work on the calendar, he wrote essays on the construction of the astrolabe and correctly observed and predicted eclipses. For Gregoras astronomy was the summit of human wisdom which 'purified the eye of his intelligence'.

## The culture of the mind and the culture of the spirit

But he, like all the Byzantine scholars of his day, retained a clear distinction between what was human and what was superhuman wisdom. They recognized a difference between what they defined as the 'outer' learning and the 'inner' learning. The former could be acquired by the study of ancient Greek literature, the 'wisdom of the Hellenes'; the latter, the 'true wisdom' could be obtained only from the Scriptures and the Fathers or through personal religious experience. The outer learning was the foundation of all higher education. But the queen of sciences was theology, in the proper sense of the knowledge of God. Theology came naturally to the Byzantines. Every respectable scholar and many an emperor tried his hand at a theological treatise or turned out some lives of saints like prize essays. Such compositions were by no means the preserve of monks and clerics. It was the concern to establish the truth of the inner wisdom that enlivened and embittered the controversy over Hesychasm. The debate reached its formal conclusion in 1351 at a council in Constantinople convened by John Cantacuzene at which Gregory Palamas was present to defend his doctrine. The patriarch at the time was a hesychast monk, a friend of Palamas and of the emperor; and the outcome of the council could be called a foregone conclusion. But the bishops there present seem to have spoken with the voice of almost all the Byzantine church when they defended the Orthodoxy of the hesychasts; and the opposition, though determined, was small in numbers. Its main spokesman was in fact Gregoras, whose obsession with theology had by then got the better of his scholarship. He died, still protesting that the hesychasts were in heresy, in 1360. He would have been appalled to know that Palamas was enrolled among the saints of the Orthodox church only eight years later.

There were some churchmen on the side of Gregoras. His theological arguments against the doctrine of Hesychasm were not baseless. But the hatred of Palamas which distorted his judgment was personal and vindictive. It was to some extent the hatred of a scholar for a mystic. It could be argued that the interest of Byzantine scholars in astronomy was stimulated by the thought that this was the science that brought man closest to his Creator. Some of them said as much. It was a bridge of a sort between the outer learning and the inner learning. Gregory Palamas, however, had a mystic's distrust of the relevance of any kind of human wisdom in the pursuit of the knowledge of God. He was far from being illiterate. He had studied philosophy and the outer learning under Theodore Metochites. His literary style had the required polish. But as a monk he believed that scholarship was behind him. It was a vain and possibly perilous distraction. Theology for the perfect monk was a matter not to be learnt from books but from revelation, from illumination, from the quest for *theosis*.

Such opinions were not to the taste of scholars like Gregoras who were engaged in rediscovering the wealth of their Hellenic heritage and piously trying to accommodate it to their received and believed religion. The way of the hesychast seemed to them to be hard and lonely. Metochites believed that monks should, so far as possible, live in society and not in the wildernesses and desert places. He furnished his own monastic foundation with a library which was open to the public. Sanctity and scholarship need not be mutually exclusive. The views of Palamas on the dangers of the 'outer' learning were extreme and not shared even by all his followers. The Patriarch Isidore, who had been his disciple on Athos (and who crowned John Cantacuzene in 1347), never forsook his love for the classics and even extolled the moral virtues of the ancient Greeks by comparison with the depravity of his own Christian society. The mingling of spiritual and temporal in the Byzantine character made it possible for a man to be a mystic and a scholar at the same time. It was even possible to trace elements of hesychast doctrine back to their platonic roots. Some of the most inspiring of all mystical literature was written by Nicholas Kabasilas who was born in Thessalonica about 1320. He was a hesychast by persuasion, the author of a commentary on the Divine Liturgy and a homily on The Life in Christ. Yet Kabasilas was a layman, at least until the close of his life, and a classical scholar who also wrote a commentary on Ptolemy; and he remained convinced of the value of learning even for the saints for, as he put it, to turn one's back on the wisdom available on this earth is to deny a part of human goodness which it is in one's power to possess.

There was room for difference of opinion about the relationship between the 'outer' and the 'inner' wisdom. But it was not in the Byzantine tradition that monasteries should be seats of learning and that monks should be scholars. In this sense Palamas was merely restoring the emphasis on the proper duty of a monk in an age when men like Maximos Planoudes seemed to be setting a fashion for monkish scholarship. The church had always allowed for two forms of the monastic life, the coenobitic and the eremitic, the communal and the solitary. The solitary, who was after all the true *monachos*, was the graduate of the long disciplinary school of communal monasticism. He was qualified to be alone with God and to find his own salvation which, as the father of monasticism, St Basil, had said, was the prime purpose of the monk. If by so doing he became revered as a holy man or a saint that was accidental.

## The revival of spirituality

Those who have been fascinated by the revival of classical learning in late Byzantium have sometimes tended to ignore the no less remarkable and contemporary revival of the spiritual life. There is almost as much hagiography in the Greek literature of the fourteenth century as there is scholarship. The holy man was still a well known and respected figure in society, living on charity but repaying his debt by his example, his miracle-working and the advice and comfort which he could impart as one who was in direct touch with God. Some of them led vagabond and rootless lives, perhaps as a result of the enforced dissolution of the monasteries of Asia Minor. But many were bred on or gravitated to Mount Athos. Hesychasm was one of the manifestations of a more general renaissance of spirituality. And here the word renaissance may be more justly applied. For the hesychast movement, carried by wandering saints, spread throughout the Orthodox world far beyond the confines of the Byzantine Empire, into Bulgaria and into Russia, creating what has been described as a 'hesychast international' which transcended political or ethnic boundaries. Hesychasm struck a far more responsive chord in men's minds in the fourteenth century than the rather precious scholarship of the literary elite; and the writings of Gregory Palamas or of Nicholas Kabasilas, though building on a deep foundation of Orthodox mysticism, are a deal more fresh and original than the pedantic antiquarianism of Theodore Metochites and his fellow scholars. In the character and career of the Patriarch Athanasios one has seen the still living force of the ascetic tradition in Byzantine monasticism. Gregoras rudely called Athanasios a hair-shirted ignoramus. Yet he admired him as a holy man. The Emperor Andronikos II was mesmerized by his patriarch. But the same emperor lavished his patronage on the scholars of the outer learning who frequented his court. In the later fourteenth century many of the patriarchs were themselves hesychast monks by origin; and their influence gave the church a much wider and more universally respected authority than the emperors could any longer command.

Hesychasm and the revival of the esoteric Byzantine spiritual life were not developments likely to improve relationships with the Roman church. Nor was the rediscovery of classical learning as a Greek monopoly calculated to promote understanding between Greeks and Latins. The classical revival was indeed partly prompted by a growing consciousness of Hellenism among the Byzantines, by a jealous pride in the fact that their exclusive possession of the legacy of Hellenic wisdom marked them off from the uncouth and illiterate Latins. But even in the time of Andronikos II there were a few scholars who were not so blinded by prejudice and who took the trouble to learn Latin, a rare accomplishment in their day. Maximos Planoudes, though chiefly celebrated for his compilation of Greek epigrams, opened a new chapter in Byzantine literature by his translations of Latin authors, among them Ovid, Cicero, Boethius and St Augustine. Planoudes was and remained an Orthodox monk and his interest in Latin literature did not extend to contemporary theology. The discovery that even western theologians might have something worthwhile to say was left to Demetrios Kydones a generation later.

Kydones came to the fore as a statesman in the 1350s and served the emperors John Cantacuzene and then John V as prime minister for nearly half a century. He was taught Latin by one of the Dominican friars in Constantinople, who set him to read Thomas Aquinas for his homework. In due course he translated the *Summa contra Gentiles* into Greek. Kydones confessed that he was amazed to find that the Latins were not all uncouth and illiterate and that it was a great mistake to judge them all by the behaviour of the Italian merchants on the Golden Horn. But above all he was carried away by the clear and logical reasoning and the beautiful certainties of the theology of St Thomas. Kydones was the forerunner of a small and select band of Byzantine intellectuals in the fourteenth and fifteenth centuries who joined the Roman church and looked to the western Christian world to save their empire from ruin. As a statesman his influence on Byzantine policy was great. As a scholar he tried to build a cultural bridge between the Greek east and the Latin west. But he knew that he was an exception to the norm. He could never carry the Byzantines with him; and the elaborate apologies which he wrote in defence of his conversion to the Roman faith betray his sense of unease at having forsworn the Byzantine if not the Hellenic part of his birthright. St Thomas Aquinas and St Gregory Palamas were branches of the same Christian root, but their blossoms were of quite different colours.

Kydones also left a large collection of letters. Many of them are little more than typical Byzantine exercises in rhetorical and literary style. But some throw valuable light on the events of what would otherwise be a comparatively dark age in Byzantine history. For it is a curious fact that the writing of history, which had always been one of the most creative forms of Byzantine literature, comes to an end about the middle of the fourteenth century. The last to compose histories of their own times were Nikephoros Gregoras and the Emperor John Cantacuzene, who wrote his memoirs after his abdication in 1354. No successor took up the tale where they left off, until 100 years later, after the fall of Constantinople to the Turks. No one living at the time seems to have had the courage to set down year by year the tragic events of the final century of the Byzantine Empire. The last Greek historians were all looking back on a world that was irretrievably lost. The revival of scholarship too, which in other circumstances might have led to a true renaissance, began to lose its impetus at about the same time. The age of wealthy patrons was over. There were some intellectual giants in the later fourteenth and early fifteenth centuries, men like Bessarion of Nicaea and George Gemistos Plethon. There were still editors and commentators of classical texts, translators and scholars who escaped to earn a living by teaching Greek in Italy. It was to such men, rather than to Akropolites, Metochites or Gregoras, that the Italian Renaissance was indebted. But the last century of Byzantium was more famous for its theological expertise than for its classical learning. The great debate of the last years was not over the defence of the legacy of Hellenism but over the defence of the Byzantine tradition in faith and theology, which some of the emperors were again prepared to compromise by seeking union with the Roman church.

The life of the spirit, however, did not lose its momentum. It was the living Orthodox tradition and not the dead classical past which was in the end to carry the Byzantine people through the trauma of the Turkish conquest and the collapse of their material civilization. The posturings of the scholarly elite made little impression on the ordinary people. But the church, vigorous in the defence of its Orthodoxy, was an everyday part of their lives; the monks were familiar figures; and the holy men were esteemed as living icons or channels of divine grace by emperors and peasants alike. The church was also a powerful social and economic force, controlling the destinies of thousands of people who worked on its estates and paid their taxes to the monasteries. In an age of great landowners the monasteries were the greatest of all; and the patriarchs, who had direct jurisdiction over the huge monastic complex of Mount Athos and its far-flung dependencies, resolutely defended the property of the church against encroachment from the state. It is no accident that nearly all the surviving documents relating to land tenure in this period derive from the monastic archives of Athos. The church unlike the state had the institutional stability to retain, document and when necessary reclaim its properties.

The church was a jealous landlord. But it was also, in one sphere at least, a generous provider or medium. The art of the late Byzantine Empire, which is the illustration of the Byzantine mind, is almost all religious in character and to be found in churches and monasteries. Some of its supreme achievements are the mosaics and wall-paintings in the church of the Chora, restored by Metochites. Some classical or humanistic influence, perhaps reflecting the tastes of the patron, may be observed in the delicate mosaic scenes in the narthex of the church. But the majestic painting of the Anastasis in the apse of the side chapel is a work of the pure Byzantine spirit. Here there is no attempt to search for the realism or perspective which Italian artists of the same generation were seeking and finding. Byzantine art to the end retained what to our eyes is its essential unreality. Its figures of Christ, the Virgin, or the saints are illumined not by the natural light of this world but by the supernatural light of the mystic or hesychast which emanates from within them, the inner light of the inner wisdom. The artists themselves, being simply the humble agents through whom the spirit was recorded, are still anonymous, though the portraits of their patrons, like that of Metochites in the Chora, are prominently labelled. We know little of the schools of mosaicists, icon-painters and craftsmen which must have flourished in Constantinople in the thirteenth and fourteenth centuries. But it is clear that the artists, like the *literati* of the age, were schooled and initiated into a style from which they deviated only in detail. The style of classical rhetoric was that which the Byzantines thought fit for the expression of their literature. This is why so much of it seems dead, factitious and uninventive. The style of their art was no less conventional and unchanging. The eternal verities which it expressed do not change. But its greater works have the merit of being charged with a live, dynamic spiritual awareness. It was through the continuing dynamism of the church as a common factor in the Orthodox countries that Byzantine artistic and cultural influences took root in Serbia, Bulgaria, Rumania and Russia in this period.

The art of the age, like the scholarship, depended upon patronage. The time came when the emperors and their courtiers could no longer afford it. Minor works such as icons and illuminated manuscripts were still commissioned. But large-scale mosaic work was far too costly for an impoverished era. There is little monumental Byzantine art or architecture in Constantinople or Thessalonica after the middle of the fourteenth century. The last flowering of Byzantine art is to be seen at Mistra, the capital of the Byzantine province in the south of Greece, where churches were still being decorated in the early fifteenth century. Mistra, the seat of the Despotate of the Morea established by the sons of John Cantacuzene, was indeed to become a Constantinople in microcosm, the last surviving centre of that blend of culture and spirituality which characterizes Byzantine civilization.

# 5 The enemy at the gate

## John V Palaiologos: the search for help from the west

In December 1354 John Cantacuzene abdicated and became a monk. In the same month of the same year his friend Demetrios Kydones finished his first translation of Thomas Aquinas. Cantacuzene had taken a great interest in the work. He was a cultured man whose mind was not closed to the best in Latin theology. But he would never try to force his people into accepting that theology and the submission to Rome which it entailed. He had had some dealings with the papacy, especially with Pope Clement VI. He had hoped that Clement would admit the Byzantines to full membership of the league of Christian powers, even though its ultimate aim was the recovery of the Holy Land and not the protection of Constantinople. But all his efforts had foundered on the pope's insistence that the Greeks must first return to the fold of Rome, renounce the schism and repent of their errors. Cantacuzene had politely held to the traditional Byzantine view that the schism could only be healed and error, on either side, identified at a general council of the church. He would make no other concessions. He would not bargain with the pope like a suppliant, as Michael VIII had done.

His son-in-law and successor John V was of a different mind. He was 22 when he became sole emperor. It was clear, once the Osmanlis had established their European bridgehead at Gallipoli in 1354, that Cantacuzene's policy towards the Turks was no longer workable. At the time the strongest power in eastern Europe, and the only power capable of driving the Turks back to Asia was the empire of Serbia. Stephen Dušan came very near to realizing his dream of mastering Constantinople. But in December 1355 he died, and his vast empire, like that of Alexander the Great, at once disintegrated into a number of squabbling successor states. John V decided that the only hope lay in appealing to the conscience of the Christians of the west. He was well placed to do so since he was related through his mother Anne of Savoy to several prominent western families. But it was to the pope that he addressed his appeal. On 15 December 1355, the week in which Dušan died, the young emperor wrote to Pope Innocent VI asking him to send a fleet and an army to Constantinople. In return he promised to effect the conversion of the Byzantines to the Roman faith and to send his son Manuel to the papal court at Avignon as a hostage. These were extravagant promises. The pope, who suspected that Byzantine affairs were incurably unstable, did not take them too seriously. He instructed his legate Peter Thomas, who was then in Serbia, to proceed to Constantinople to interview the emperor; and there the matter rested. The league of Christian powers was in fact reconstituted at Smyrna in 1357. But once again the Byzantines were left out of account. Pope Innocent died in 1362 and direct negotiations between Byzantium and the papacy were not resumed until two years later.

John V meanwhile pinned his hopes on the Latins nearer home. The Genoese had always supported his family. They were rewarded with possession of the island of Lesbos and full control of Chios. The Venetians too were encouraged to renew their treaty. But only a substantial army could drive back the Turkish flood pouring into Thrace from Gallipoli, and this the emperor was unable to muster. Orchan's son Suleiman had given leadership and direction to the bands of Turkish warriors already roaming the land. In 1359 some of them broke through to the walls of Constantinople. Others penetrated into northern Thrace and as far inland as Philippopolis (Plovdiv), which they captured in 1363. Suleiman died in 1359 and his father Orchan in 1362. The new emir of the Osmanlis was Murad, and for some years he was occupied in defending his Asian territories against his own brothers. The Turks in Europe did not relax their offensive; but once again it lacked direction. This might have been a moment for the Byzantines to rally their strength and fight back. But John V was not the man to seize the moment; and there was little unity of purpose among the neighbouring Orthodox kings and princes, for all the efforts that the patriarch made to bring them together.

In 1364 the emperor heard that a new crusade was being planned by Pope Urban V. Among those who had taken the cross were his cousin Amadeo of Savoy and the King of Hungary, Louis the Great. In the event neither went with the crusade, which ended in disaster at Alexandria. But Hungary was the nearest Catholic neighbour of Byzantium and John V naively hoped that its great king, as a committed crusader, might be moved to help him by a personal appeal. In the winter of 1366 he set out for Hungary with two of his sons. No Byzantine emperor had ever before sunk his pride and his dignity to pay court to a foreign monarch. It had always been assumed that it was the part of lesser princes to come to the one true emperor at Constantinople. John V could not afford to stand on his dignity. His journey set a precedent which was to be much followed. The affair was doubly humiliating, for nothing came of the visit and on his return the emperor was detained at the frontier between Hungary and Bulgaria. The Bulgarians would not allow him to travel through their country. The one true emperor was the captive of his Christian neighbours.

During his absence, however, his cousin Amadeo of Savoy had unexpectedly arrived at Constantinople. The pope had given his blessing to this enterprise on condition that Amadeo would do all he could to bring the emperor and the Greeks over to the Roman church. As Kydones observed at the time, a show of practical assistance was more likely to work this miracle than any number of emissaries from the pope. Amadeo did his best. In August 1366 his little armada attacked and captured Gallipoli, driving out the Turks. When he reached Constantinople he learnt of the plight of his cousin the emperor. At once he sailed up the coast of the Black Sea and bullied the Bulgarians into releasing their captive and allowing him to cross their territory. Amadeo had no money left for further military ventures. But he did not forget his promise to the pope. He had with him a papal legate, Paul, lately bishop of Smyrna, whose mission it was to persuade John V of the advantages of union with the Roman church. Back in Constantinople in 1367 discussions took place. John himself needed little persuasion, but he knew that he could speak only for himself and for a few intellectual converts like Demetrios Kydones. If the pope's legate was to be properly briefed, someone in authority must be found to put the Byzantine case to him. The patriarch refused to take any part in the discussions. John therefore invited his father-in-law, John Cantacuzene, to come out of his monastery and to hold a dialogue with Paul of Smyrna. A record of this interview has survived. The Byzantine case had not changed. Cantacuzene emphasized, as he had done before, that real unity in the church could never be a matter of political expediency. Nor could it be achieved by the simple fiat of a pope or an emperor. The many differences between Greek and Latin Christians could only be resolved at a fully oecumenical council attended by the pope, the patriarch and all their colleagues and principal subordinates. Only at such a gathering would the Holy Spirit inspire them with truth and lead them to true unity.

## The emperor's conversion

The papal legate is said to have agreed to put this proposal to the pope. A council would be arranged in Constantinople within two years. The patriarch began to send out invitations. But Amadeo was more realistic. Before he left for Italy he made the Emperor

John V promise that, in any event, he would make his own submission to the pope as a penitent convert in person. The emperor was blackmailed into handing over some jewels and other securities which he could redeem as soon as he had fulfilled this promise. As a crusader Amadeo knew, and he was right, that the pope would never authorize military aid for the defence or rescue of Constantinople until its emperor acknowledged his obedience to the Holy See. Papal priorities were the same as they had been in the days of Clement IV and Michael VIII: repentance must come before rescue. By restoring Gallipoli to the Byzantines Amadeo had given them a foretaste of what might follow if they renounced the schism.

The recovery of Gallipoli was in fact the greatest service rendered by Amadeo of Savoy. It was to remain in Byzantine control for about ten years and the Turks were prevented from sending further reinforcements across the Straits to Europe. The Byzantines themselves had hardly the will or the strength to make the most of this advantage. The co-operation of the Christians in the west might have turned the tide. But that co-operation never came. Nothing more was heard of the project to hold a council of the church. The pope's response was a spate of letters assuring the Greeks of the benefits of becoming his obedient servants. Finally, in 1369, the emperor was persuaded to fulfil his promise to go to Rome. He left his eldest son Andronikos in charge of Constantinople and his second son Manuel in Thessalonica. With him he took Demetrios Kydones, who had translated the documents required by the pope. But not a single member of the Byzantine hierarchy felt like joining him. In October, at an impressive ceremony on the steps of St Peter's in Rome, the pope, surrounded by his cardinals, received the humble submission of the 'Emperor of the Greeks', who had abjured the errors of his Orthodox faith and freely professed the creed of the Holy Roman Church. John V's conversion was a private and personal affair. Not even the pope pretended that a union of the churches had occurred. He only prayed that the emperor might have set an example for other Greeks to follow. The Byzantines too were inclined to be generous about the emperor's idiosyncracy so long as their church and faith were unaffected.

On his way home the emperor stopped at Venice. It was the wrong place to look for sympathy. The Venetians reminded him that he was already heavily in their debt. They were, however, interested in his proposition to sell them the strategic island of Tenedos at the entrance to the Hellespont. Instructions were sent to Andronikos in Constantinople to arrange the deal. But Andronikos refused to obey the order, doubtless under pressure from the Genoese. In the end John had to be saved from his predicament by his other son Manuel, who sailed from Thessalonica to Venice with enough money to bail his father out. The matter of Tenedos remained unsettled. But John V got back to Constantinople in October 1371. He had been away for nearly two years and he had little to show for his pains. He must have seen while in Italy that the Latin Christians were divided among themselves and that the pope was in no position to mount a crusade. The news that met him on his return was no comfort. Adrianople, the chief city of Thrace, had fallen to the Turks in 1369. From there they had driven deep into Macedonia. The Serbians who had joined forces against them had been annihilated in a battle on the Marica river less than a month before, in September 1371. The Turks were now demanding the return of Gallipoli.

## The Ottoman advance into eastern Europe

The battle at the Marica in 1371 was the most decisive victory yet won by the Turks in Europe and perhaps the most consequential of all their triumphs before they delivered the *coup de grâce* in 1453. It opened the gates into Serbia, Macedonia and northern Greece. Two of the heirs of Stephen Dušan had been killed. The other Serbian princes were now required to pay tribute and to fight alongside their Turkish masters when summoned. The pattern was set of Christian vassalage to the Muslims. The Bulgarians were soon forced to the same condition. The Byzantine emperor would be the next. He had little choice. Constantinople was now very nearly isolated by land and the chance of any army fighting its way through from the west seemed smaller than ever. His second son Manuel, who bravely held on to Thessalonica and its neighbourhood, showed more spirit than his father. But his eldest son Andronikos, who had already proved uncooperative, rebelled and joined up with a son of Murad who also had a grievance against his father. The rebellion was soon put down. Murad, who was furious at this Byzantine-Turkish insubordination, arrested and blinded his son and commanded John V to do the same. Andronikos was put in prison, though not irremediably blinded. His imperial title was taken from him, however, and given to his brother Manuel, who was crowned as co-emperor in September 1373. By then the Emperor John V had affirmed by treaty his humiliating status as a vassal of the Sultan, for such was the high title which Murad now claimed. The Osmanli emirate of Bithynia was well on the way to becoming the Ottoman Sultanate or Empire.

It is hard to discern the causes of the joint revolt of the sons of Murad and John V. But its consequences gave still more scope for the enemies of Byzantium to achieve their purposes by fostering the feuds between members of the imperial family. In 1376 Andronikos escaped from prison into the arms of his friends in Galata. From there he made contact with Murad; and with the active help of the Genoese and the Turks he fought his way into Constantinople and arrested his father and brothers. Whatever his motives, Andronikos had now put himself and the empire heavily in debt. The Turks required as their reward not only the payment of more tribute but also the return to them of Gallipoli. The deal was done and the Ottoman territories in Europe were now once again firmly linked across the Hellespont to those in Asia Minor. By 1377 Murad was so sure of his control of the Straits that he set up his first European capital at Adrianople, henceforth to be known as Edirne. The reward which the Genoese demanded for their services was the island of Tenedos at the entrance to those straits. Andronikos would have granted it, had not the Venetians already occupied the island. The Byzantines were thus thrown into another round of conflict between Genoa and Venice. The disputed possession of Tenedos was only a symptom of their rivalry. It was the starting point of a war on a much larger scale; and the major battles in that war were to be waged in Italian waters far from Constantinople, until the contenders fought themselves to exhaustion in 1381.

From 1376 to 1379 there were four crowned emperors of the same family in Constantinople: Andronikos IV, his son whom he had crowned as John VII, John V and his son Manuel II. The last two were in prison, but Andronikos who had put them there was scarcely more master of his own fate than they. All were in a sense agents of Turkish or Italian policy. It was the feebleness of the father Emperor John V which had allowed this to happen. In June 1379 he and his son Manuel escaped from the clutches of Andronikos and went straight to the sultan's camp across the water. There was nowhere else that they could go. Murad was pleased to be given another chance to act as kingmaker. The Venetians were glad to provide ships to turn the usurper out of Constantinople. The Turks supplied the necessary army; and in July John and Manuel re-entered the city. Andronikos fled again to his Genoese friends in Galata, cruelly taking with him as hostages his mother and his elderly grandfather John Cantacuzene. For over a year the rival emperors then fought out their feud across the Golden Horn between Constantinople and Galata, the Venetians and the Turks siding with John V, the Genoese with Andronikos IV. The fighting ended only when John agreed to reinstate Andronikos and his son as heirs to the throne and allotted them an appanage in Thrace. Manuel, now abruptly disinherited, took himself off to Thessalonica, the city which he had governed before; and there, as if disgusted with all his family, he set himself up as emperor in his own right.

His brother Theodore was sent out to Greece to take over as Despot of the Morea from the last of the Cantacuzenes.

By 1383, the year when John Cantacuzene died in the Morea, the fragments of the empire appeared at last to be held together as a family concern, with John V in Constantinople, Andronikos IV in Thrace, Manuel II in Thessalonica, and Theodore Palaiologos in Mistra. But it was a quarrelsome family whose senior member had no policy but to appeal for help from the west and to appease the Turks. Only Manuel showed any initiative. For nearly five years, in defiance of his father and of the sultan, he made Thessalonica a rallying-point for resistance and for reasserting Byzantine authority in Macedonia and Thessaly. It was a heroic gesture, but it came too late. The sultan's troops encircled the city. Many of the inhabitants, well aware of the fate that lay in store for cities that resisted the Turks, were for surrendering. Manuel finally despaired of turning them into heroes and left them to themselves. In April 1387 the gates of Thessalonica, second city of the Byzantine Empire, were opened and the Turks marched in.

The vendetta between John V and his son, which he had done so much to promote, gave the Sultan Murad a free hand to organize his conquests. With Gallipoli once more in his control and with a capital established at Adrianople, he was able to bring more troops across to consolidate his European territories. It was Murad who laid the foundations of the Ottoman Empire in the Balkans on which his successors were to build. As in Asia Minor the native inhabitants were encouraged to join the Osmanli fold. But every non-Muslim subject was bound to pay the *haradj* or poll-tax, whatever immunities he may have enjoyed before. Landowners employing large numbers of peasants were particularly penalized, for they were held responsible for any defaulters. The monasteries with their great estates could no longer expect to be exempted. The monks of Mount Athos, sensing the wind of change, had prudently made their submission to the sultan in 1386. He respected their autonomy. But they had to pay the *haradj* not only on their own account but also on account of the many properties which they owned in far-flung parts of the Orthodox world. Turkish immigrants and settlers were also deliberately imported into Europe. Conquered lands were divided into fiefs among the soldiers and into feudal domains among the officers. But Murad also had at his command numerous levies of troops which his Christian vassals in Serbia, Bulgaria or Byzantium were bound by treaty to supply; and he took to recruiting prisoners-of-war into his infantry, some of whom were selected for his personal use. This private guard of the sultan was to evolve into the famous regiment of janissaries or 'new troops', formed of Christian youths, which was to play so significant a part in the history of the Ottoman Empire. The *ghazi* warriors of Islam were encouraged to press on with the holy war against the infidel at the limits of the sultan's dominions. But at the centre a solid basis of government, administration and Muslim religious and educational institutions was being laid. It was this talent for transforming a mobile warrior state into a stable institution that distinguished the Osmanlis from the other Turks.

The speed of the Turkish conquest was phenomenal. After the battle at the Marica in 1371 their armies moved systematically up the river valleys into Macedonia, Bulgaria, Serbia and over to Albania. Sofia fell in 1385, Niš in 1386, Thessalonica in 1387. The capture of Niš, however, stimulated a new resistance from the Serbians. Their leader was Prince Lazar, who had organized a coalition of other Serbian magnates and allied with his neighbours in Bosnia. They contrived to halt the Turkish offensive in 1388 and the news of their success inspired a wider rebellion. The Bulgarians were emboldened to tear up their treaty with the sultan. The Wallachians north of the Danube in Rumania were eager to assist. The sultan dealt with them in characteristically methodical fashion. First the Bulgarians were chastized. Trnovo, their capital, and then Nikopolis were attacked in 1389, and their tsar was relegated to his former status of a vassal. Murad then arrived in Europe in person and led his army into Serbia, collecting levies from his Christian vassals as he went. On 15 June 1389 Prince Lazar with his Serbian and Bosnian army met the Turks on the plain of Kossovo north of Skoplje. It was a memorable encounter which quickly became romanticized in Serbian folklore. In the heat of the battle Murad was killed, but his command was immediately assumed by his son Bajezid who led the Turks on to a devastating victory. Lazar was captured and executed. Legend set the number of Serbian dead at 77,000. Legend is a potent force. It can turn defeat into a moral victory. When the news of Murad's death reached the west men gave thanks in the churches, in France and in Italy, for the triumph of the Cross over the unbeliever. The real outcome of the battle of Kossovo was that Serbia had now become a client state of the Turkish empire. Lazar's son, Stephen Lazarević, was permitted to be its native ruler, but only on terms of total subservience to the Turks.

The Turkish mastery of the situation was made evident at Kossovo by the sight of Serbians, of Christians, on both sides in the battle. But there was no Byzantine contingent. Nor had there been eighteen years before when the flood gates were first opened after the battle at the Marica. The Byzantines could not agree among themselves let alone co-operate with their Slav and Orthodox neighbours. The best that their emperor could offer them was the fond hope that an army would come to their rescue from the west. But the Turkish victory at Kossovo had completed the isolation of Constantinople by land. Resistance to the Ottomans was now more effectively broken in Europe than it was in Asia Minor. But the new sultan Bajezid was determined to impose his authority in both continents. The other emirates in Asia were to feel the full force of that determination as he ruthlessly incorporated them into his empire. Murad had assumed the title of Sultan. Bajezid wanted to be known as the legitimate 'Sultan of Rum', the ancient title held by the Seljuq princes of Anatolia. Thessalonica was already his. The conquest of Constantinople would inevitably follow. He believed it to be ordained by Allah.

## Byzantium at the mercy of the Ottoman Turks

Bajezid was even more adept than his father at weakening Byzantine resistance by playing cat and mouse with the various contenders for the throne. The first agent of his schemes was the young John VII, whose father Andronikos IV had died in 1385. In April 1390 he helped John to seize control of Constantinople. The Venetians in the city at the time reported that they expected the sultan to arrive at any moment and take control himself. But in September Manuel managed to throw out the usurper and to restore his father John V as emperor. Bajezid did not like being outwitted. He ordered the payment of more tribute and summoned Manuel to his camp in Asia Minor, bringing soldiers with him to fight for the Ottoman Empire. John VII had already obeyed the same summons. Two of the rival claimants to the Byzantine throne were thus safely in the sultan's custody; and in the autumn of 1390 both were obliged to assist him in the siege and capture of Philadelphia, the last remaining free Greek city in Asia. It was the ultimate humiliation.

In anticipation of the worst, John V added some new fortifications to the walls of Constantinople. The sultan now commanded him to pull them down; otherwise he would hear that his son Manuel had been blinded. The emperor could do no more. He shut himself up in his palace and died a few months later in February 1391. He was not yet 60. He had reigned, on and off, for 37 years, long years in which everything had gone from bad to worse. There was far less to show at the end of his reign than there had been at the beginning. In 1354 there had still been a recognizable Byzantine Empire, at least in Europe. In 1391 the process of its transformation into an Ottoman Empire was already far advanced. In days long gone by the Byzantines had believed in the eternity of their empire as a divinely protected society destined to last until the Second Coming of Christ. In their bewilderment at the end of the fourteenth century some took comfort from the reflection that there was not long to wait for the Second Coming. There were books of prophecy that set the event at the end of the sixth millennium, which on Byzantine reckoning would be the year 1492. Then the survivors would be gathered up in glory and all their enemies be confounded. Others were less hopeful and less gullible. Even in the time of Andronikos II, Metochites had proposed the shocking theory that the Byzantine Empire was perhaps subject to the same historical process that had caused other empires to come and go. This theory implied that another empire would take its place, for the Byzantines found it hard to envisage any alternative form of government. In other words, their enemies would not be confounded. They would triumph. The last Byzantine historians, who all lived after that triumph had been won in the fifteenth century, recognized that this was the fact. The Christian empire had given place to a Muslim empire with the Sultan-Basileus as its emperor. But in 1391, when there was still hope of a miracle, this was too hard a pill to swallow.

The hope of a miracle was fostered by the church. People may well have lost confidence in their emperors, and they had plenty thrust upon them in the fourteenth century. But they seldom lost faith in their church. Their patriarchs and bishops had a ready answer to the question, why had God forsaken his chosen people and allowed them to be so humiliated? It was because of their sins, because they had left the paths of righteousness and turned to wickedness. If they would repent and mend their ways then they would find the courage and the strength to defy their enemies. The Turkish conquests were God's chastizement of the sinful Christians. Sermon upon sermon drove the message home. People felt cheered by the thought that other men were so wicked. On the other hand, the church stubbornly and consistently clung to its material wealth. Only the Emperor Manuel, when in Thessalonica, had the courage to expropriate some of its estates for military purposes. The leaders of the church were affronted by such behaviour. Yet church and empire still went together in men's minds. The one could not exist without the other. The point was forcibly put by the Patriarch Antony IV in 1393 in a letter to the Grand Duke of Moscow, Basil I. The dukes of Moscow owed no political allegiance to Byzantium. But the spiritual bond was strong and it had been customary to commemorate the emperor's name in their churches. Basil I had presumed to let this custom lapse on the grounds that 'we have a church but no emperor'. The patriarch, whose authority extended over the Russian church, was quick to put him right. The empire, he wrote, might be sadly reduced. The enemy might be at the gates of its capital. But the emperor was still God's regent on earth, the anointed of God, the superior of all other Christian princes, the visible head of the universal church of true believers. To most Byzantines these eternal truths were still self-evident even in the dark days of the turn of the fourteenth century. It is significant, however, that it was left to the church to enunciate them. An emperor such as John V could hardly have found the confidence.

The Patriarch Antony performed the coronation of John's successor in 1392. The new emperor was Manuel, known as Manuel II. It had been touch and go. Manuel had been at Prousa when the news of his father's death reached him. He slipped away from the sultan's camp by night and made for Constantinople before his nephew John VII had time to act. Bajezid was angry. He had wanted to select his own emperor who would be indebted to him. He retaliated with new demands. The Byzantines were now to admit a resident agent of the sultan in Constantinople and to provide special facilities for Turkish merchants. The payment of tribute was to continue. Only three months later the new emperor was summoned back to the sultan's camp. Most of the first year of his reign was passed serving with Bajezid's army on the march in Asia Minor. But Manuel was a man of greater character and stamina than his father. He was indeed more the grandson of John Cantacuzene than the son of John Palaiologos. He had inherited Cantacuzene's taste for literature and theology; and he whiled away his bitter hours in the sultan's camp by writing sophisticated letters to his friends, among them Demetrios Kydones. He even held debates with Muslim theologians, which he was later pleased to record in literary form. Kydones acclaimed him as the long-awaited philosopher-king. The title, though rhetorical, fitted Manuel II better than most Byzantine emperors. Even the sultan was impressed by the regal bearing and presence of this tall, handsome, bearded figure. He was already 40 when he came to the throne and in 1392, when he was released from the sultan's service, he married a Serbian princess who was to bear him six sons. In other circumstances such an emperor, his dynasty so well secured, might have left his mark on history. It was tragic that Manuel was never given the scope to exercise his many talents. He came into a *damnosa haereditas*.

The sultan allowed him to go back to Constantinople, but with a warning. 'If you disobey my commands', he said, 'then shut the gates of your city and govern what lies behind them; for everything beyond the gates belongs to me.' It was almost true. In 1393 the Bulgarians, spurred on by the King of Hungary, made a bid for freedom. It was ruthlessly stifled. Their tsar was executed and his capital of Trnovo was occupied by the Turks. Bulgaria now became the first fully constituted province of the Ottoman empire in Europe, its people no longer the vassals of the sultan but his subjects. Its administration was to set the style for the other European provinces of Turkey. Shortly afterwards Bajezid summoned all the remaining Christian rulers in the Balkans to his presence at Serres in Macedonia. Among them were the Emperor Manuel, his nephew John VII, his brother the Despot Theodore from Mistra, and two Serbian princes. The sultan meant to break their nerve. He let it be known that he had it in mind and in his power to murder them all. But having so graphically demonstrated who was master of their fate, he let them go. The experience confirmed Manuel's suspicion that Bajezid was deranged and no longer open to reason or negotiation. The next time that he was summoned to the sultan's camp he sat tight behind the walls of Constantinople.

Those walls had been the despair of every enemy of Byzantium since the fifth century. Only the crusaders had succeeded in breaching them and that from the sea. Bajezid had few ships and, as he well knew, little chance of storming the walls from the landward side. But he could perhaps starve the inhabitants into surrender. In the spring of 1394 his soldiers burnt and destroyed the outskirts and the first real blockade of Constantinople began. It was to last for about eight years. There was famine and despair in the city. There was even talk of capitulation. From the walls people could see the sultan's engineers constructing a fortress on the Asiatic side of the Bosporos, the castle of Anatolia or Anadolu-Hisar, whose walls still stand. From here Bajezid planned to direct his assault on Constantinople. Italian ships occasionally got through with shipments of food; for it was possible to beat the blockade by sea. The Venetians even offered to take the emperor away to safety. The grim reports which their captains brought home gradually made some impact in the west.

## The crusade of Nikopolis: the Emperor Manuel II's journey to the west

The conquest of Bulgaria too had alerted the King of Hungary to the danger on his doorstep. It was he who took the first practical measures to organize a Christian counter-offensive, by appealing to all the crowned heads of Europe, the pope in Rome and the pope in Avignon. Their blessing turned the venture into a crusade, the last of the international crusades on the grand scale. France and Hungary played the main part. Charles VI of France sent about 10,000 men. Sigismund of Hungary led his own army of 60,000. Smaller units from Wallachia, Poland, Bohemia, Italy, Spain and England made the total up to about 100,000. The Teutonic knights and the Knights of St John joined in, as well as the Genoese from

Lesbos and Chios; while the Venetians, after some prevarication, provided ships to patrol the Hellespont. In August the crusaders set off down the Danube valley. There was much disagreement about their plans and their objective. The sultan on the other hand knew exactly what he was doing. He was ready for them near Nikopolis in Bulgaria; and there on 25 September 1396 their vast army fell into his hands. King Sigismund escaped, but most of the other leaders and their men were massacred.

The crusade of Nikopolis was the first trial of strength between the nations of western Europe and the Ottoman Empire. Its principal object had been the protection of Catholic Hungary, though the French crusaders had dreamed romantic dreams of harrying the infidel all the way to Jerusalem. As a distraction to the Turks, it brought a momentary relief to Constantinople. But Bajezid resumed the blockade of the city as soon as he was able. The Emperor Manuel had not been much in the crusaders' minds. But at least he could now be sure that the Latins had seen the real strength of the enemy and hope that they would listen to his calls for help with greater understanding. He pressed home his advantage by writing to the pope in Rome, to Venice and to the kings of France, England and Aragon, as well as to the Grand Duke of Moscow. All the world must know the danger that threatened if Constantinople were allowed to fall to the Turks.

The King of France had lately acquired a new interest in the east. In 1396 he had become suzerain of the Republic of Genoa and so of the Genoese colonies in Byzantium. John VII, or so it was rumoured, even offered to sell his imperial title to the French king. Among the French prisoners taken at Nikopolis was the Marshal Boucicaut. He had been ransomed and returned to his country with a terrible tale to tell. He longed to go back and smite the infidel. Charles VI authorized him to go to the Emperor Manuel, whom he had already met, taking a body of 1,200 soldiers; and in 1399 the brave Boucicaut, like Amadeo of Savoy, broke through the Turkish blockade by sea and arrived at Constantinople. He was welcomed as a hero and the emperor joined him in a number of skirmishes against the enemy beyond the walls. But both of them knew that the relief of the city needed a whole army and navy. Boucicaut therefore advised the emperor that he had better go back with him to France and state his own case to the king. Manuel agreed. It meant leaving Constantinople in charge of his contentious nephew John VII, but this too the marshal tactfully arranged. In December 1399 Manuel set sail for Italy. More than three years were to pass before he returned.

Manuel must often have heard his father's tales of woe about his own travels to Hungary, Rome and Venice. John V had travelled cap in hand like a beggar. Manuel travelled in style with an impressive retinue and he had the presence and the personality to win respect as well as sympathy. The western world had certainly become more alive to the menace from the Turks. But in Italy at least there was now a new interest in things Greek. In 1396 the emperor's friend Manuel Chrysoloras, a pupil of Demetrios Kydones, had been appointed to teach Greek at Florence. Educated Italians were eager to meet Byzantine scholars as purveyors of the new enlightenment of classical Greek learning; and Manuel was a fine advertisement for it. There was nothing beggarly about his behaviour or abject about his entreaties; nor did he offer as an incentive the conversion of himself or his people to the Roman church. He asked only for the unconditional help of fellow Christians.

His first port of call was in the Morea in the south of Greece, to leave his wife and family in the safe keeping of his brother Theodore. From there he sailed to Venice and so by way of Padua, Vicenza, Pavia and Milan he reached Paris in June 1400. Charles VI received him with the greatest honour and promised to send him another army under Marshal Boucicaut. In December the emperor crossed over to England, where King Henry IV received him no less courteously. Everywhere he went Manuel was given a royal welcome and was led to expect great things. From London he wrote to his friend Chrysoloras praising the magnanimity of Henry of England, who was going to raise an army and a fleet for the rescue of Constantinople. The pope in Rome had also set up a fund offering indulgences to all who subscribed. Back in Paris in February 1401 Manuel settled down as the guest of Charles VI. He spent his time writing literary and theological essays, one of them in defence of Orthodox doctrine against its French detractors. Only slowly did it dawn on him that all the promises of help from England and even from France were inflated and illusory. The crowned heads of Europe had their own problems nearer home. Even Marshal Boucicaut's zeal had waned. He left to become governor of Genoa in 1401.

## The battle of Ankara: the Turks defeated by Mongols

All the while Manuel's nephew John VII was holding the fort in Constantinople supported by the French troops that Boucicaut had left there. The city was still under siege, still without food and without much hope. But then the miracle happened. News came through as early as 1400 that the Mongols had invaded Asia Minor. The Sultan Bajezid had long been aware that the Mongols were on the move, inspired by a leader who saw himself as the second

Genghis Khan. His name was Timur and he had made his headquarters at Samarkand, whence he carried his conquests in all directions, against the Golden Horde in Russia, against the Ilkhans of Persia, and into India. The name, and the legend, of Timur were also already known in Byzantium and in the west. Embassies had been exchanged to try to provoke the Mongols into alliance with the Christians against the Turks. John VII sent a messenger to Timur to propose that, if he defeated Bajezid, the Byzantines would transfer their tribute to him. When he had overrun Georgia and Armenia, Timur came face to face with the Ottomans. In 1400 his army destroyed Sivas (Sebaste) on the sultan's eastern borders. This was simply by way of a warning. The Mongols then turned on Syria and on Baghdad which fell to them in July 1401.

Bajezid was not a man to take heed of warnings. He boasted that an upstart like Timur could not so lightly tempt the vengeance of the lord of the universe. In the spring of 1402, stung by the taunts of Bajezid, Timur marched into Anatolia by way of Sivas. The sultan staked all on a pitched battle; and on 28 July 1402 the Ottoman and Mongol armies met near Ankara. The Christian levies on the sultan's side, among them the Serbians, fought with more conviction than the Turkish troops; for the Mongols were Muslims by faith, and by Islamic standards it was hardly a holy war. The sultan and his 10,000 janissaries fought bravely to the end. But the victory went decisively to Timur. Bajezid was captured and died as a prisoner. Legend had it that he was carried around in an iron cage. It is certain that he had to endure the sight of the upstart Timur marching at will through his dominions. The Ottoman Empire, at least in Asia, was shattered. The Mongol hordes, notorious for their savagery, swept through it like locusts, until they reached the coast.

At the time no one knew what Timur's next move might be or whether he might turn his hordes loose on Europe. His defeat of Bajezid meant that the blockade of Constantinople was over. But even the Byzantines held their breath to see which way the conqueror would go. He withdrew as suddenly as he had come in 1403. Only then was it clear that the hoped-for miracle had happened. On the anniversary of the battle of Ankara, on 28 July 1403, the Byzantines in Constantinople gave thanks, where they believed thanks to be due, to the Virgin, the protectress of their city, for delivering them from the infidel.

# 6
# Into captivity

## A last respite for Byzantium

The news of the miracle at Ankara reached the Emperor Manuel in Paris in September 1402. He composed a prayer of thanksgiving of his own. But it was to be nearly a year before he got back to Constantinople for he stopped at Genoa and Venice on his way. In the meanwhile his nephew John VII had made his own arrangements to deal with the changed situation. Constantinople was free of the blockade for the first time for eight years. The fearsome Sultan Bajezid was no more. But his four sons survived to dispute the succession; and it was with them that the Byzantines had to deal. The eldest of them was Suleiman, and he forestalled his brothers by getting to Gallipoli in August 1402 to take command of the European provinces of the shattered Ottoman Empire. There a summit conference was held and early in 1403 a treaty was signed by John VII, Suleiman and representatives of Genoa and Venice. The terms were unbelievably favourable to Byzantium. Thessalonica with Mount Athos was restored to them, as well as a long stretch of the Black Sea coast and some of the Greek islands; they would pay no more tribute to the Turks; and Suleiman swore to become the emperor's vassal. In return he was to be recognized as Sultan of the Ottoman dominions in Rumelia or Europe with his capital at Adrianople. The Italians too derived some profit from this treaty. But the Byzantines did best. From being the impoverished subjects of the Turks they were now their overlords, with much of their lost empire given back to them. It remained for the senior emperor Manuel to ratify the agreement. This he did in June 1403 shortly after his return. He made one new condition, however. John VII was to leave Constantinople and reign as emperor in Thessalonica. This could have been either a reward or a punishment; but it underlined the fact that, even after four years separation, Manuel II and John VII could not live together in the same city.

For some years after 1403 Manuel was able to turn the tables on the Turks, playing at kingmaker among the rival members of the sultan's family. Suleiman had three brothers, each of whom saw himself as the one who would reunite the Asiatic and European sections of the Ottoman Empire. The Byzantines could not fail to take sides in the fratricidal struggle. Their interest lay in siding with Suleiman who had behaved so generously to them. But his brother Musa waged a long and bitter war against him until, in 1410, Suleiman was defeated at Adrianople and killed. Musa then turned on those who had befriended his brother, annulled the treaty of 1403, attacked Thessalonica and laid siege to Constantinople. Manuel had foreseen this possibility, however. Constantinople was well prepared for a siege; and he invited Mehmed, now the only surviving brother of Suleiman, to come over from Asia Minor. Mehmed failed at his first attempt. But in 1413, at the head of an army augmented by Byzantine and Serbian troops, he drove Musa out of Adrianople and ran him to ground in Serbia. By process of elimination Mehmed I thus became Sultan of Rumelia and of Rum, of Europe and Asia. He had been led to victory by the Byzantines. He was sincerely grateful and at once rewarded them by confirming the treaty which Suleiman had made ten years before. He would be like a dutiful son to his father the emperor. So long as Mehmed was sultan, from 1413 to 1421, that agreement was honoured. But Manuel was wise enough to see that it could not last for ever. Like the arrangements which his grandfather had made with the Turks, it was based on a personal relationship, a gentlemen's agreement. It gave the Byzantines a respite. Manuel determined to make the best use of it. It was the last respite they were ever to know.

Manuel was still hopeful that his kind hosts in the west would remember him and send some of the financial or military assistance which they had promised. He appointed his friend Manuel Chrysoloras as his ambassador at large to keep the western world alert to the danger in the east. Economically the empire was richer by the amount it had formerly paid in tribute to the Turks; and the emperor decreed that all landowners, lay and monastic, must continue to make over to his treasury in Constantinople one third of the *haradj* which they had been paying to the sultan. Much of the proceeds was spent in laying in stocks and strengthening the defences of the capital against the day when the respite would be over. The government of what was left of the empire beyond the capital seemed to be well under Manuel's control. In 1408 John VII died, thus laying the ghost of a long family feud, and Manuel appointed his own son Andronikos as his deputy in Thessalonica. He made another of his sons governor of Mistra in the Morea. Manuel rightly regarded the Despotate of the Morea as his most promising outpost of empire. His brother Theodore Palaiologos died there in 1407 after 25 years of successful administration and defence. The emperor went to Greece to read his funeral oration in person; it was a well-deserved tribute. Theodore, continuing the good work begun there by the sons of John Cantacuzene, had survived both Latin intrigue and French aggression. In 1397 central and southern Greece had had their first taste of invasion by the Turks, who temporarily captured Athens, sacked Argos with deliberate brutality and overran the Morea. They had not stayed, however; and under the new agreement with the sultan after 1403 the Despotate had again become prosperous and secure. Manuel meant to keep it that way. In 1414, having made his peace with the new Sultan Mehmed, he visited Greece again. He spent the winter in Thessalonica and then sailed down to the Morea. His plan was to ensure the defence of southern Greece against Latins and Turks alike by building a wall across the Isthmus of Corinth. The work was done quickly and the wall, known as the Hexamilion, turned the Morea into a Byzantine island, at least for a few more years.

## The Byzantine Despotate in the Morea

The administrative capital of the Morea was Mistra, set on the foothills of Mount Taygetos above the ancient Sparta. By the early fifteenth century Mistra had become, like Constantinople a hundred years before, a focus of learning, art and culture. It was filled with churches, monasteries, palaces, schools and libraries. The court of its despots had become a haven for scholars, monks and artists where patronage, albeit on a limited scale, could still be offered. Among those who lived and worked there in the last years were the monk Isidore, later bishop of Kiev, who was to be made a cardinal of the Roman church; Bessarion of Nicaea, also to become a cardinal; and George Scholarios, the future Gennadios II, the first patriarch of Constantinople under the Ottoman Empire. Mistra could have become the centre of a Byzantine political and military revival. But there was, as Manuel complained, an uncontrollably quarrelsome spirit among the native inhabitants of the Morea. 'It seems to me', he wrote, 'that it is the fate of the Peloponnesians to prefer civil war to peace.' The local Greek landlords were happier feuding among themselves than settling down under a central government imposed upon them, as they thought, by despots and administrators from Constantinople.

The fact that it was on Greek soil, however, engendered a fancy that Mistra might become the breeding-ground of a new Hellenism, a centre of ancient Greek philosophy and ideals which would reinvigorate the ailing spirit of Byzantium. This idea was enthusiastically promoted by the philosopher George Gemistos Plethon who lived and taught at Mistra in the early fifteenth century. Plethon convinced himself that the Byzantines were the spiritual heirs if not the direct descendants of the ancient Greeks. Earlier scholars had toyed with this fancy and had taken to calling themselves Hellenes instead of Romans, or Byzantines. But Plethon constructed a whole programme on his hypothesis, a programme of reform of the government, the economy, the social structure, the agriculture and the defence of the island of the Peloponnese as the nucleus of a new Greek or Hellenic state. He outlined his proposals in a series of addresses to the emperor and the despot. There was some sense in his propositions, although the authoritarian regime which he envisaged was more Spartan than Athenian, more dictatorial than democratic.

His scheme was striking because of its suggested innovations. Plethon was the only Byzantine philosopher who proposed a radical change in the order of society, the only true social reformer. His audience listened politely, applauded and let the matter drop. But when Plethon carried his innovations into the realm of religion the reaction was not so mild. Late in life he composed a treatise called *On the Laws* in which he advocated that Christianity should be rejected in favour of a new 'Hellenic' religion based on a theological and philosophical system concocted from Plato with a dash of Zoroastrianism. The ancient Greek deities were to be resuscitated as more fitting to Hellenes than the God of the Christians. In many ways, especially in his platonism, Plethon was the intellectual heir of Theodore Metochites. But no Byzantine before him had ever dared or wanted to push his Hellenism so far. In this sense he was an original thinker, a rarety in Byzantium. But he was not representative of his society, and it was that society which finally condemned him. His atheistic or anti-Christian tract was burnt by his friend George Scholarios when he became patriarch, as a perverse and dangerous document. Plethon found more honour in Italy than in his own country. As an academic Hellenist and platonist he was to be received as a founder member of the Platonic Academy in Florence; and though he died in Greece his mortal remains were later to be transferred to a more glorious grave in Rimini.

The Hexamilion wall across the Isthmus of Corinth and the repaired defences of Constantinople advertised the truth about Byzantine-Turkish relations. The Sultan Mehmed was a man of his word, but the Emperor Manuel took no chances. He well knew that the Sultan was putting together the pieces of the Ottoman Empire in Asia Minor on new and firmer foundations and that he had built a fleet. There were moments of tension. In 1415 a pretender to the sultanate called Mustafa, who claimed to be a son of Bajezid, was given asylum by the emperor when on the run. When Mehmed tried to intervene his new fleet was destroyed off Gallipoli by the Venetians. The emperor now had in his hands a

Turkish pretender who might prove useful in the future. But his agreement with the sultan was not seriously impaired. Neither party was yet ready to break that agreement by an act of war. Yet there were those on both sides who felt that the days of gentleman's agreements were past and that some action was required. The Venetians had shown the way by sinking the sultan's ships. The opportunity for action soon came.

## The renewed Turkish offensive

In January 1421 Manuel II, now aged 71 and in poor health, handed over most of his authority to his eldest son John VIII, who had been serving in the Morea with his brother. Four months later the Sultan Mehmed died at Adrianople. His son Murad II claimed the succession. Manuel would have recognized his claim, but the activists in Constantinople, now led by the young John VIII, put up the pretender Mustafa for the sultanate in the misguided belief that the Byzantines could still behave as puppet masters to the Turks. Murad quickly showed them their mistake by coming over from Asia Minor and capturing and murdering the pretender. He too felt that the time for action had come and in June 1422 he set his army to lay siege to Constantinople. Revenge on the treacherous Greeks was in his mind; but his objective was nothing less than the conquest of the capital city, the missing link in the chain of his Eurasian empire. The siege of 1422 was the most determined assault so far made on the city. A Muslim prophet foretold that it would fall on 24 August. But not even Murad's determination could break down the walls, and in September he withdrew his troops. Once more the inhabitants, who had fought back heroically, gave thanks to their protectress, the Mother of God. But they knew that their respite was now at an end. On Murad's orders, other Turkish armies were invading Albania and Epiros, blockading Thessalonica and marching into Greece. They made short work of the Hexamilion wall, stormed into the Morea and ravaged the country. A settlement was reached in February 1424. But it was very different in kind from the agreement between Manuel and Mehmed. The emperors were now again reduced to ruling what lay behind the walls of their city and obliged to pay tribute to the sultan for the possession of their throne. Beyond the city little but Thessalonica and the Morea remained to them, the one under siege, the other battered by invasion.

Thessalonica, now cut off by land from Constantinople, was held by Manuel's son Andronikos. He was young and an invalid. In his desperation he offered to make over the city to Venice. The Venetians hesitated and then accepted the offer. It was a cession rather than a sale, made with the approval of the Emperor Manuel and with the knowledge and disapproval of the sultan. In September 1423 the Venetians sent governors to administer Thessalonica. Andronikos left to join his brother in the Morea, where he died four years later. The Venetians, who had brought badly needed provisions for the starving citizens, boasted that they would transform Thessalonica into a second Venice. But they could not convince the sultan of their good intentions. Murad demanded ever larger amounts of tribute; 30,000 of his troops continued to blockade the city; famine raged inside it; and the Greek inhabitants threatened to open the gates to the Turks unless their needs and their interests were better served by their Italian masters. After seven years the Venetians concluded that Thessalonica was a liability which they could no longer afford. In March 1430 Murad personally commanded the assault that broke its defences. The Venetians sailed away and the second city of the Byzantine Empire fell into Turkish hands for the second and last time. It would have done better to surrender than to resist. The Turkish soldiers, in accordance with Islamic law, were given licence to ransack its houses and churches; and 7,000 of its citizens, about one fifth of its population, were carried off as slaves.

Manuel II did not live to see the second conquest of the city which had once been his personal empire. He died in July 1425, leaving his son John VIII as sole emperor. After Murad's attack on Constantinople, John had travelled to Venice, Milan and Hungary in another effort to solicit help from the west. He achieved little. But he was convinced that the end could now only be averted by a rescue operation from the western world; and to bring that about he was prepared to make the compromise which his father had rejected by proposing the union of the churches. In his old age Manuel had warned his son against this policy: it would make the Turks suspicious and it would upset and antagonize the Byzantines. But John could see no alternative. The best that he could do was to insist that the union should be realized in the manner most in accord with Byzantine tradition. There must be an oecumenical council.

## The Council of Florence: union of the churches

Circumstances were unusually favourable for such a proposal. There was now a party in the western church which argued that the authority of a council was greater than that of the pope, an argument somewhat in line with Byzantine feeling. In 1431 the conciliarists, as they were called, met at Basle. In the same year Pope Eugenius IV was elected. The Emperor John VIII was probably not well-informed about the dissensions in the Roman church, but it was natural for him to address himself to the pope. For all their distrust of the universalist claims of the papacy, the Byzantines still regarded the pope as the leader of western Christians and they could not envisage a church without a Bishop of Rome as one of its patriarchs. The conciliarists, hearing what was afoot, invited the emperor to send delegates to their assembly at Basle, pointing out that they and not the pope represented authority in the church universal. There was nothing to be lost by hedging his bets; and in 1433 the emperor dispatched three legates to Basle. Thereafter the matter developed into a race between the pope and the conciliarists to win the favour of the Greeks for reasons of prestige. Both parties sent their own ambassadors to Constantinople to put their case. The Byzantines had never been so flattered and courted by the western church; and the concession that they gained in the end was one which no pope had ever before allowed them. Pope Eugenius, having won over a minority faction of the conciliarists, agreed to summon a council of his own at Ferrara in northern Italy. The emperor was invited to bring his patriarch and bishops to discuss and, if possible, resolve the causes of the schism in the atmosphere of an oecumenical council. This concession settled the matter. The emperor accepted the invitation. The pope at once sent ships to fetch the Byzantine delegation. He did well to act quickly, for the conciliarists had also sent ships to Constantinople to take the delegation to their alternative council at Basle. But the emperor had made up his mind; and in November 1437 he and his company embarked on the pope's fleet to sail to Italy. He had already recalled his brother Constantine from the Morea to take charge during his absence.

No such Byzantine delegation had ever gone to Italy before. This was to be a very different event from the Council of Lyons in 1274 or the personal conversion of John V in 1369. The Patriarch Joseph II was elderly and ill, but he was willing to go with his emperor, and he prevailed upon his three colleagues, the patriarchs of Alexandria, Antioch and Jerusalem to send their representatives. Other distinguished members of the party were Bessarion, bishop of Nicaea, who had studied with Gemistos Plethon at Mistra; Isidore, bishop of Kiev, who had been one of the delegates to Basle; Mark Eugenikos, bishop of Ephesos; George Scholarios, later to be patriarch; and Plethon himself. All told there were about 700 persons. The cost of their travel and maintenance in Italy would be formidable. But their expenses were to be met by the pope, who thought it a small price to pay for so great a moral and diplomatic victory over the conciliarists.

The unionist party in Byzantium had gained some ground in

previous years, inspired by the followers of Kydones. But they were still a small minority; and they were inclined to an intellectual acceptance of the Roman faith and doctrine which was not to the taste of most Byzantines, whose Orthodoxy came from the heart and not the head. This made them well fitted, however, for the debates at the council which were conducted on the Latin side with a wealth of well-prepared intellectual argument of a kind unfamiliar to most of the Greeks. Those debates and disputes at Ferrara and then at Florence, to which the council moved in 1439, were long and sometimes bitter. They make tedious reading and are of rather more interest to the historian of the church than to the historian of the Byzantine Empire. It is hard nowadays to believe that the arguments about whether the Holy Spirit proceeds from the Father and the Son or from the Father alone should have occupied so many great minds for so many months. The other main points of divergence between the churches, the use of unleavened bread in the Sacrament, the Latin doctrine of Purgatory, and even the question of the primacy or supremacy of the See of Rome, were all tactfully resolved or circumvented. They were of course familiar, perhaps too familiar. Each side had enshrined or ossified them in polemical tracts for centuries, tracts entitled Against the Latins or *Contra errores Graecorum.* Under pressure of circumstances the Byzantines could give way on some of them. But the problem of the Holy Spirit was the dearest to their hearts, for they had always sincerely believed that the Catholic addition to the Creed made a muddle of the delicate relationship between the persons of the Trinity and so of theology or the knowledge of God. At an oecumenical council, such as the Council of Florence purported to be, the Holy Spirit was supposed to inspire those present with the truth. All the more important to reach agreement about the Spirit's nature. A compromise formula was in the end discovered after months of wrangling. It was reached by blurring the distinction between the prepositions 'from' and 'through'. The Byzantines agreed that the Holy Spirit proceeded from the Father 'through the Son', which could be taken to mean 'from the Son'.

By then most of them were weary of it all and nostalgic. The aged patriarch had died before it ended. The Emperor John VIII had worked hard to control his delegation and to prevent them from being too bitterly disputatious. He still believed that the salvation of Constantinople depended on the successful outcome of the council. At length a document was drawn up. It was signed by both parties, and on 6 July 1439 the union of the Greek and Roman churches was formally proclaimed and celebrated. The pope gave his blessing and the decree of union was read first in Latin by Cardinal Cesarini, who had led the debate on the Roman side, and then in Greek by Bessarion of Nicaea. The heavens were invited to rejoice that the wall which had divided Christendom for 437 years was now demolished. The emperor returned to his capital more hopeful than ever before that his reward would be a crusade.

His homecoming was not a happy event. He must have known his people better than to think that they would welcome him as a hero. But he might have expected some gratitude. His unhappiness was compounded by the news that his beloved wife had died a few days before. The reaction in Constantinople to the Union of Florence was not unlike that which had followed the Union of Lyons 165 years earlier. The men who had subscribed to it found themselves denounced as traitors. The only bishop who had refused to sign it, Mark Eugenikos of Ephesos, was lionized as a confessor for the faith. He was quickly recognized as leader of the opposition. Others who had signed it soon changed their minds when they got home. One was George Scholarios who, though an admirer of Thomas Aquinas and deeply interested in Latin theology, came to feel that he had betrayed the faith of his fathers. The issue naturally expressed itself in politics. The emperor's brother Demetrios was unsuccessfully put up by the anti-unionists, with Turkish support, as the new emperor who would restore Orthodoxy. The convinced unionists, like Bessarion of Nicaea, could not compete with the emotional outcry stirred up by the fanatical Mark of Ephesos. Bessarion, who had already been made a cardinal of the Roman church, left Constantinople for Italy at the end of 1440, never to return. The hostility was no less fierce in other parts of the Orthodox world. Isidore of Kiev, whom the pope had also made a cardinal, was loudly condemned and arrested as a traitor when he went back to Russia. He too escaped to Italy. The emperor did his best to put the union into practice. A patriarch was found who would conscientiously commemorate the pope's name in his services in St Sophia, though the other eastern patriarchs disowned the signatures of their representatives and rejected the union. The Sultan Murad was angry and suspicious of the practical consequences that might follow from the event. All seemed to have fallen out much as Manuel II had warned that it would.

## The crusade of Varna

Pope Eugenius had promised, once the union was proclaimed, to preach a crusade. He was as good as his word. Once again the natural starting point was Hungary. By 1440 the Turks had penetrated deep into northern Serbia. The last of the Serbian princes, George Branković, had built a huge fortress at Smederevo on the banks of the Danube near Belgrade. He had given his daughter in marriage to the Sultan Murad, but he was not spared on that account. Smederevo was taken by the Turks in 1439 and Belgrade, after a long siege, in the following year. Branković took refuge with his ally, Ladislas III of Hungary and Poland. Ladislas was fortunate in having with him a brilliant and courageous general who had already crossed swords with the Turks, the Hungarian John Hunyadi. The pope looked to them to lead the promised crusade to Constantinople. The arrangements and the propaganda for it were committed to Cardinal Cesarini. It took some years to mature. But by 1443 all was ready. The moment was propitious for the sultan had been called away to Asia Minor; and there were signs of Christian resurgence in Europe. In Albania a rebellion against the Turks was being fired by a renegade Muslim called George Kastriotes. He was so formidable a warrior that the sultan himself had given him the nickname of Alexander or Skanderbeg. In the Byzantine Morea too there was new hope in the air. The emperor's brother Constantine repaired the Hexamilion wall across the Isthmus and forced the Italian lord of Athens to pay him tribute.

In these promising circumstances, the crusade from Hungary set out in July 1443. It followed much the same route as the crusade of Nikopolis. The army of about 25,000 men led by Cesarini, Branković and Hunyadi went down the Danube valley, while the fleet was to sail up the Black Sea to meet them on the coast. Niš and then Sofia were retaken from the Turks. These were notable successes and they alarmed the sultan. In 1444 he hurried back to Europe and persuaded the leaders of the crusade to sign a truce for ten years. Its terms were ratified by King Ladislas in July and Murad felt free to return to Asia Minor in the belief that his enemies, being Christians, would not break their oaths. He had misjudged them. George Branković felt bound to observe the truce. The other leaders were at odds among themselves; but Cardinal Cesarini convinced them that they should make the most of their advantage. In September therefore the army continued its march through Bulgaria to the Black Sea. The sultan was shocked at their perfidy. He rushed back across the Bosporos and in November arrived at Varna with an army at least three times as large as theirs. He went into battle with the text of their broken treaty fixed to his standard; and there at Varna on 10 November 1444 the crusade was routed by the Turks. Ladislas of Hungary and Cardinal Cesarini were killed. Only John Hunyadi escaped.

The crusade of Varna was the last concerted attempt by western Christendom to relieve Constantinople. But it never came within sight of the city. The Byzantine emperor had taken no part in it and his people had no cause to give renewed thanks to the Virgin. Some of them indeed believed that the Virgin had already withdrawn her protection from her city as a consequence of the Union of Florence. How could she continue to work miracles for a people who had falsified their faith? The failure of the crusade played into the hands of the anti-unionists by proving the point that the Byzantines were not going to be saved by adulterating their creed and compromising their beliefs to suit the pope. Some even felt and said that losing their liberty to the Turks would be less odious than purchasing it from the Latins. Thousands of Christians had now been living under Muslim rule for a generation or more. They could compare the rough justice and tolerance of their Turkish masters with the arrogance and high-handedness of the French and Italians in their Greek colonies. Life was hard under the Turks, but many would rather have stability and permanence than face the uncertainty of liberation, preferring the ills they had to the unknown quantity of a freedom bought with Latin help.

Murad soon took his revenge on those who had assisted the crusade or had thought to profit from it. In 1446 he marched into Greece, destroyed the Hexamilion wall and for a second time let his soldiers loose in the Morea. It was only a punitive raid but the province was left ruined and depopulated. 60,000 prisoners were taken away as slaves; and the Despot Constantine and his brother Thomas were now bound under oath as vassals of the sultan. Murad then turned to the punishment of John Hunyadi and Skanderbeg. Hunyadi, who had now become regent of Hungary, still dreamed of leading another crusade. But Murad caught up with him at Kossovo in October 1448. Resistance in the Balkans was now nearly at an end. George Branković, alone of the leaders of the crusade of Varna, survived as the sultan's vassal until his death in 1456. He had learned better than most when to be a hero and when to opt for prudent neutrality. Skanderbeg of Albania, by contrast, earned the glory of being the last Christian hero of them all, defying the Turks in his rugged mountain country until he died in 1468.

## The last Byzantine emperor

For the Emperor John VIII in Constantinople the choice between heroism and neutrality was not open. Neither the one nor the other could now save the city from the Turks. The crusade for which he had paid so dear a price at Florence had failed; and he had earned himself the distrust or contempt of most of his people. In October 1448 he died, without hope and without an heir. He had nominated his brother the Despot Constantine to succeed him. As might almost have been expected in the family of Palaiologos, however, two of his other brothers disputed Constantine's right to the throne: Demetrios who was the champion of the anti-unionist party and

Thomas who represented nothing but himself. Only the firmness of the dowager Empress Helena, mother of them all, saved the day. She asserted her right to act as regent until Constantine arrived in the city from the Morea. Constantine liked to be known by his mother's Serbian name of Dragaš or Dragases. He was, after John VIII, her favourite. He was crowned emperor at Mistra in January 1449. Following the precedent of Michael VIII and John VI, who had both been crowned in the provinces, he may have thought to set the seal on his coronation with a later ceremony in Constantinople. But to be crowned by a unionist patriarch in St Sophia, which so many of the Orthodox now refused to enter, would not have been diplomatic. As it was, the Patriarch Gregory III, whom John VIII had appointed, found the task of reconciling his flock to the Union of Florence so impossible that he abandoned them and went to Rome in 1451. For the last two years of its Byzantine life Constantinople had no patriarch to perform a coronation. But in any case time was short. Constantine XI Dragaš Palaiologos was the last Byzantine emperor.

The Sultan Murad was dutifully informed of the change of emperor and made no objection. He was getting old and tired and had already delegated most of his powers to his young son Mehmed. If he did not live to see Constantinople added to his empire, his son would. He had made certain of that. In February 1451 Murad died and Mehmed came into the full inheritance and the certain hope for which he had been carefully schooled. From the very start he made it plain that his heart was set on the conquest of Constantinople. The Byzantines soon knew that all the prophecies were about to be fulfilled and that the end of their world was at hand. But at first they looked on the bright side. Mehmed was only 19 years old. People in the west too were lulled into thinking that not much harm could be done by so young and untried a sultan who seemed pleased to extend his good will to them by treaties. The new emperor was tactless enough to suggest that Mehmed might increase the amount of maintenance money which his father had been paying to a pretender to the sultanate who was living in Constantinople. Otherwise the pretender might be let loose. Mehmed had some worries with rebellious elements in Asia Minor. But he would not have the Byzantines playing games with him. Those days were long since past. This incident convinced him that he must now teach them their final lesson.

In the winter of 1451 Mehmed revoked the small concessions which he had made to the Byzantines and gave orders for the encirclement of Constantinople to begin. A massive fortress was erected on the European shore of the Bosporos in sight of Constantinople. It came to be called Rumeli-Hisar, the European castle, standing as it still does across the water from the Asiatic fortress of Anadolu-Hisar built by Bajezid. It was finished in August 1452. From here the siege and final capture of the city were to be planned and launched. The main obstacle to the success of the operation was the same as it had always been, the strength of the walls of Constantinople, particularly on the landward side. Mehmed knew those walls intimately. He had burnt the midnight oil studying plans of them. He knew too that the Byzantines could throw a chain across the entrance to their harbour, the Golden Horn, so that his ships could not sail in to attack the sea walls. But Mehmed also knew more than his enemies about the new weapons of artillery, and he could afford to pay for them. When his father had invaded the Morea in 1446, he had taken cannons with him. The science of heavy artillery warfare was not yet far developed, but the sultan was fortunate in having pre-empted the services of a Hungarian engineer called Urban who had mounted a gun on the ramparts of Rumeli-Hisar. This proved its worth by sinking a Venetian ship that tried to run the blockade in the Bosporos. Urban was commanded to construct a cannon twice its size which would be rolled all the way from the foundry in Adrianople to the land walls of Constantinople.

Against such weapons the Byzantines stood little chance. They might have done better to bow to the inevitable, remembering what had happened to Thessalonica in 1430. But Constantinople was the Queen of Cities, the New Jerusalem, the symbol of all that was left of their ancient glories. They could not let it go without a fight. In the domestic conflicts of their imperial family in the previous hundred years there had always been a party inside the city favourable to one contender or the other. The rival emperors had not had to batter down the walls to get in. No doubt there were a few at the end who favoured surrender to the sultan and who would have opened a gate for him. If there were, they kept their thoughts to themselves. In the last weeks the general mood was overwhelmingly for resistance. The chance that rescue might yet arrive from the west continued to inspire some feeble hope. The Emperor Constantine encouraged the pope to feel that the Council of Florence had not been in vain. Pope Nicholas V, who had succeeded Eugenius in 1447 and who was a friend of Bessarion, complained that the emperor had not tried hard enough to make his people see the benefits of the union of the churches. He can only have meant spiritual benefits since the material advantages were scarcely evident.

In 1452 the pope appointed Cardinal Isidore to go to Constantinople as his legate. He brought with him a body of 200 archers from Naples. Perhaps they were intended to be the forerunners of a larger army which would come when the Greeks were seen to have submitted to the pope's authority. For Isidore's real mission was to proclaim and to celebrate the Union of Florence in their midst in Constantinople. In December 1452, after much heated argument, he had his way. The sound of Turkish guns in the Bosporos persuaded some of the anti-unionists to change their tune and a service was held in St Sophia in the emperor's presence, a combined celebration of the Orthodox and Catholic liturgy. The decree of union as signed at Florence was read out and the heavens may once again have rejoiced. But the event brought little joy to the people. George Scholarios, now the monk Gennadios, who had passionately argued against it, pinned a manifesto on the door of his cell testifying before God that he would sooner die than desert his Orthodox faith. The union was an evil thing which would surely bring God's wrath upon them all. Having delivered his last warning on the subject Gennadios held his peace. His hour was to come some months later, when the wrath of God had clearly been visited upon his people.

## The siege and capture of Constantinople by the Turks

The story of the last siege and capture of Constantinople has often been told. There will always be those, especially if they are Greeks, apt to be moved to tears by its telling. It is a tale of courage and of tragedy, which touches the emotions even of those in the far continent and islands of western Europe. If the prospect of it had been so moving a hundred years before it happened, there might have been no cause for tears and a different tale to tell.

The peace in the church, solemnized by the combined Greek and Latin service in St Sophia at the eleventh hour, made little impression on the practical businessmen of Venice and Genoa. Venice was doing a brisk trade with the Turks. A change of masters in Constantinople might make it brisker; though the Venetian islands of Negroponte and Crete had to be protected. Genoa too was watching to see which way the trade winds would blow, and her colonists in Galata were instructed to preserve a cautious neutrality. The only western ruler who showed an active interest in Byzantium at the end was Alfonso V of Aragon and Naples. The pope supported him, but Alfonso's true ambition was to revive the Latin empire of Constantinople to which he believed he had a claim. Nothing could have been less realistic or relevant to the occasion. When the occasion came, however, the Venetians resident in the city willingly joined in its defence; and some Genoese came from Italy of their own accord, notably the gallant and experienced soldier Giovanni Giustiniani who was given command of the land walls with his own company of 700 men. It was a small and belated recompense for all the wrongs that the Italians had done to Byzantium in the past. The emperor was glad to have them, though he had to use all his tact to stop them quarrelling among themselves.

The number of the Greek and foreign defenders of the city was not more than about 7,000. They had to hold the walls against a force at least fifteen times as strong, the core of which was a finely disciplined army of some 60,000 men, commanded by a single-minded sultan with his 10,000 janissaries, and supported by fourteen batteries of guns each comprising four cannons. The largest gun the world had even seen had been dragged from Adrianople by 60 oxen and stationed with the rest in firing range of the land walls. It was there that the main assault was to be directed. The sultan had ensured that Constantinople was for the first time completely cut off by sea as well as by land. His fleet was stronger than ever before and patrolling the mouth of the Bosporos. Even if his guns, his soldiers and his ships failed to break the defences, the Byzantines would sooner or later have to choose between surrender or starvation.

On Easter Monday, 2 April 1453, Mehmed sent an advance guard to pitch camp outside the walls. At least the Byzantines had been spared to celebrate and to gain spiritual comfort from their Easter ceremonies. Three days later the sultan arrived with the rest of his army. The first bombardment of the walls began on 6 April. The roar of the great cannon and the smaller guns was terrifying in its intensity. Much damage was done, but during the night the defenders were able to creep out and make hasty repairs. On the other side of the city the Turkish fleet was driven off when it tried to break through the chain which had now been fixed across the Golden Horn. Three Genoese ships and a cargo vessel full of supplies fought a passage through the Turkish lines, and the boom was lifted to let them in. The Byzantines began to take heart. But the sultan now realized that his blockade would never be complete until his own ships were inside the harbour. He must have them transported overland from the Bosporos, up and over the hill behind Galata and down into the Golden Horn. It was a vast and complicated manoeuvre, but Mehmed had the manpower and the materials to achieve it; and on the morning of 22 April the Byzantines and their allies looked out in horror and dismay at ship after Turkish ship being launched into their harbour from the other side. There were about seventy of them. The Genoese at Galata, who might and probably could have sunk them all, watched and waited.

The defenders had been thinly enough scattered along the four miles of the land wall. They now had to stretch their strength to patrol and hold the sea wall as well. An attempt was made to set fire to the Turkish ships but it failed. Stocks of food were dwindling in the city; nerves and tempers were beginning to fray. In February Venice had finally promised to send some reinforcements. But in April there was still no sign of them. The Venetians and the Genoese quarrelled and brawled. There were angry incidents between Greeks and Latins. Many of the Greeks turned on their emperor and reviled him as one who had brought them to this pass by his abuse of their faith. The daily pounding of the walls by gunfire was enough to break their morale. But even the heavens seemed to be saying that all hope was lost. A strange light was seen above the dome of St Sophia. The most holy icon of the Virgin when brought out in solemn procession slipped from its framework; a thunderstorm broke out that deluged the streets with rain and hail; a dense fog descended on the city. But in the last days the Emperor Constantine, whom some of them despised, was to be the life and soul of their resistance. Before he planned his final assault, the sultan offered the emperor terms of surrender if he would evacuate the city. Constantine replied that he and his people would rather die. The sultan could have anything else he wanted, but not the city of Constantinople. It was the last communication between a Byzantine emperor and an Ottoman sultan.

Mehmed was now able to address his troops with the welcome words that, under the laws of war, they would have the right to three days plunder as soon as the city was in their hands. Parts of the outer wall on the land side were already in ruins beyond repair. It would not be long before a breach was made in the inner wall. The sultan began his final preparations on 27 May. The next day his troops rested. Even the guns were silent, and the unwonted hush from the Turkish camp preyed on the defenders' nerves. They now knew that the hour of crisis was upon them. The emperor harangued his people and his allies urging them to hold fast. Icons and sacred relics were carried round the city and all the church bells were rung. In the evening those who were not manning the walls gathered in the cathedral of St Sophia. Now that the barbarians were really at the gate a sense of common danger impelled Greeks and Latins to pray together, to ask that the Holy Spirit would descend, whether through or from the Son, to give them courage. Orthodox and Catholic bishops, priests and monks joined in the celebration of the Divine Liturgy. The Emperor Constantine was there and the Cardinal Isidore. It was a greater miracle than all the councils of the church had been able to work. When he had confessed and taken Communion, the emperor went back to his palace and then rode into the night to make a last inspection of the walls.

The expected assault began in the early hours of Tuesday 29

May. The Turkish soldiers charged in successive waves, as they had been instructed. Giustiniani had command of the weakest section of the wall and for a long time held the breach. At the same time other Turks attacked the sea walls, but there too the line was held. The sultan's plan was to give the Christians no respite. Each new wave of his soldiers was fresh and eager. He kept his janissaries to the last. By the time they came rushing forward yelling their battle cry, the defenders had been fighting without rest for more than six hours. Just before daybreak Giustiniani was wounded in the chest and forced to retire. His troops at once lost heart and the janissaries saw their chance. Some of them beat their way through to the inner wall and scaled it. But another company of Turks had already broken in to the city through a little gate in the wall, climbed a tower and planted the Ottoman standard. The janissaries recognized the signal and pressed their attack, some through the gaps in the wall, others through the open gate. The defenders were surrounded with no way of escape. But the emperor was in the thick of it, still trying to rally them. At the last the Byzantine Empire was reduced to a muddy patch of land by the gate of St Romanos in the city of Constantinople where a handful of brave men, the emperor prominent among them, fought hand to hand with the Turks. It was there that the Emperor Constantine was last seen. He had thrown away his regalia. He was killed fighting as a common soldier against the invincible might of an enemy who had, for a century and more, been steadily whittling away the measure of his inheritance.

Once the Turks were inside the walls, the Christian cause was lost. The soldiers on the ramparts left their posts to look to their own safety. The Venetians rushed to their ships, weighed anchor and, having smashed the boom across the harbour, sailed off at speed, their decks packed with refugees. A number of Genoese ships followed them, some carrying members of the Byzantine aristocracy, Palaiologi and Cantacuzenes, who had found time to collect their families and flee from the wrath to come. Some made for Chios, some for Crete and some for Venice; they were the forerunners of the Byzantine diaspora which was to bring so many Greek exiles to the Venetian colonies or to Venice itself after 1453. They were lucky to escape the wrath. Even if the Turks had spared their lives they would have had little left to live for in Constantinople. The sack and plunder of the city, which the sultan had promised to his victorious troops, lasted for three days and nights. Private houses, churches and monasteries were ransacked and destroyed; the imperial palace was gutted; books and icons were stripped of their precious bindings and silver frames and thrown on to bonfires. The Turks murdered every living thing that stood in their way. The streets ran with blood. They had heard that the richest loot of all was to be found in the cathedral of St Sophia. The janissaries were the first to get there. The great church was packed with terrified people who had fled there as if by instinct. They had bolted the doors but the soldiers soon broke their way in and began to tear down the precious ornaments and to seize their captives. There was no escape for the victims and the building rang with the screams and tears of men, women and children being slaughtered or rounded up as slaves. The conquering Sultan Mehmed entered the city as soon as all resistance was over and rode at once to St Sophia to give thanks. One of his priests mounted the pulpit to intone the praise of Allah and his Prophet, and the sultan then made his own prayer to the God of Islam who had singled him out to fulfil the ancient prophecy that Constantinople would one day be a Muslim city.

When his soldiers were sated with plunder, Mehmed made inquiries about the fate of the more distinguished prisoners. He was especially anxious to make certain that the Emperor Constantine had not survived or escaped. Many conflicting tales were told of the manner of the emperor's heroic death. But there was no doubt that he was dead. The sultan was relieved. The last Constantine would not become a living symbol of hope for the Christian cause. The sultan also sought out those members of the aristocracy and ruling families who had been captured. Most of them were executed. They too were safer dead than alive, though their wives and children were either taken into the seraglio or settled at Adrianople. Some of the prisoners whom Mehmed would like to have seen managed to get away, Cardinal Isidore among them. But there was one for whom he had a particular task in mind.

When the shouting and the tumult died the sultan needed a man who would be answerable to him for the conduct of the whole Christian community within his empire. The obvious candidate was the patriarch of Constantinople, for it had been proved that the Byzantine church as an institution had at the end shown greater staying power than the state. The appointed patriarch, however, the unionist Gregory III, was in Italy. A new one must therefore be found who would, unlike Gregory, command the loyalty and obedience of his Christian flock. The sultan's choice fell on George Scholarios, the monk Gennadios. A search was made and he was found working as a prisoner in the house of a Turk at Adrianople. Gennadios was formally elected patriarch by such bishops as could be assembled and accepted the daunting responsibility of serving his conqueror as head of the self-governing community or *millet* of Christians within the Ottoman Empire. In January 1454 he was enthroned as the Patriarch Gennadios II, not in the cathedral of

St Sophia, which had been turned into a mosque, but in the church of the Holy Apostles. His staff of office was handed to him by the emperor, as was the tradition – or rather by the sultan, who now saw himself as the Sultan-Basileus, the heir by right of conquest to all the Caesars and all the Constantines.

# Conclusion

### The last outposts of Byzantium

After 1453 the only portion of the Byzantine Empire still held by the family of Palaiologos was the Morea. Now that he was master of Constantinople, Mehmed was in no great hurry to go to the trouble of taking it from them. The Despots of the Morea were after all his vassals. But his hand was forced by the behaviour of the Greeks themselves, by the innate propensity for civil war among the local landlords, of which Manuel II had complained, and by constant fighting between the Despots Thomas and Demetrios, brothers of the late Emperor Constantine. In such an atmosphere of rivalry and disunity there was never a chance that Mistra might fulfil its promise of becoming a new Athens or Sparta, the centre of a new Hellenism, as Plethon had dreamed, nor even that it might develop into the nucleus of a Byzantine Empire in exile. After a number of costly and fruitless military interventions the sultan lost patience with the Greeks; and on 29 May 1460, seven years to the day since the fall of Constantinople, Mistra was made to surrender. The fact that it succumbed without a struggle says little for the courage of its inhabitants. But at least it was spared destruction, with the result that the ruins of Mistra stand to this day as the best preserved example of a late Byzantine city. Athens had already been taken from its Italian lord in 1456. The Turkish conquest of the rest of the Morea was completed in 1460. Thomas Palaiologos fled to Italy to be comforted by the pope and by Cardinal Bessarion. He died in 1465. Demetrios went to the sultan's court at Adrianople and died as a monk in 1470. It was through the offspring of Thomas, some genuine some perhaps spurious, that the line of Palaiologos was perpetuated in western Europe for several generations; and the marriage of his daughter Zoe or Sophia to Ivan III of Russia in 1472 raised from the ashes the double-headed eagle of the Palaiologi and added some substance to the growing myth that Moscow was the Third Rome.

The last of all the tattered remnants of Byzantium was the little Empire of Trebizond whose rulers, though far removed from Constantinople and generally outside the main stream of events, had continued to call themselves emperors since the time of the Fourth Crusade. Theirs was hardly an empire in the territorial sense, being confined to a strip of coast on the southern shore of the Black Sea. But constitutionally they were proud to bear the title of Emperors of all the East and to claim descent from the imperial family of Komnenos. From time to time the emperors in Constantinople tried to call them to heel or to bring them within the larger family by intermarriage. Their chief link with Byzantium was through the church, as the number of unmistakably Byzantine churches and monasteries in and around Trebizond still testifies. But for the most part Trebizond lived a life of splendid if precarious independence and isolation, Byzantine in manners and Greek in language. It maintained itself partly by being a port where the Venetians and the Genoese could do profitable business, partly by a judicious policy of submission to its powerful inland neighbours, the Turks and the Mongols. Its emperors were never above buying peace from the half-tamed chieftains of the surrounding Turkish or Mongol tribes by giving them as a bride one of their providentially plentiful and proverbially beautiful daughters. They were patrons of art and learning too. The scholars of Trebizond were especially well placed to collect and translate mathematical and astronomical works from Persian and Arabic sources. Like Byzantium they did well out of the defeat of the Turks at Ankara in 1402, for they had fought on the Mongol side. But once the Ottomans had reasserted their right to the whole of Anatolia they could not let a Christian empire, however small and insignificant, continue to exist on their territory. The desperate efforts of the later emperors of Trebizond to form an anti-Turkish coalition only made the sultans more than ever determined to be rid of them. In 1460 the Sultan Mehmed put his great mind to the problem; and in August 1461, faced with destruction by an immense Turkish fleet and army, the last emperor of Trebizond handed over his city. He was taken into honourable captivity at Adrianople. But two years later he and his family were executed. Like the emperors of Constantinople they were safer dead than alive.

The Italians who had done so much to sap the strength of the Byzantine Empire lived off its carcase for a little longer. The Genoese at Galata had expected some thanks from the Turks for their neutrality during the final siege. They were disappointed. Chios and a few other Greek islands remained in their control until 1566. But long before that Genoa had lost all its trading posts and colonies in the Black Sea. The Venetians held on more tenaciously to some of their possessions in Greek waters; but they were constantly fighting a rearguard action against the westward advance of the Turks, until all that was left of their great commercial empire was Corfu, the island nearest of all to Venice. The island of Crete, however, which they held until 1715, had a special significance as a haven or a halfway house for Byzantine émigrés to the west and as the breeding-ground of a form of Greco-Italian culture which expressed itself in art and literature. Crete was the home or the refuge of many of the Greek scholars who were to help collate the texts and feed the printing-presses of Venice with classical manuscripts in the years after 1453. Few of them were geniuses. The great days of the transmission of Greek culture to Italy had begun nearly a century before with Chrysoloras and reached their climax with Bessarion and Plethon. Manuel II's visit to the west and then the Council of Florence had stimulated cultural exchange. Those were the days when Italian scholars too had come to Constantinople to drink at the fount, humanists like Guarino da Verona or Francesco Filelfo, who married into the Chrysoloras family. Aeneas Sylvius, the future Pope Pius II, believed that no aspiring scholar could complete his studies without a visit to Constantinople. But the interest of Italian humanists was in the glorious past of ancient Greece not in the melancholy present of Byzantium. The clouds of glory trailed to Crete or to Italy by the Byzantine émigrés were those of Plato, not those of Palamas. When Aeneas Sylvius heard of the fall of Constantinople he wept, not so much for the stricken spirit of Christian Byzantium as for 'the second death of Homer and Plato'. The dispirited refugees from the city soon learnt that their most saleable commodity in the west was not their Byzantinism but their Hellenism, not their inner but their outer learning.

## The causes of the Empire's death

The causes of the fall of the Byzantine Empire were many. One was undoubtedly old age. It had outlived its place in history. Its inhabitants were generally resistant to change or innovation. They were slow to see that their institutions could not survive without adapting to the changing circumstances of the world about them. They preferred to cling to their outmoded ideology of a world empire long after it had ceased to bear any relation to reality. They were living in the past. Their scholars in the fourteenth century were content to rediscover the ancient foundations of Greek learning. They fought shy of building anything new upon those foundations. Their merchants quickly abandoned the struggle to compete with the new methods and aggressive enterprise of the Venetians and the Genoese.

The rot in the social and economic structure of Byzantium was already far advanced in the twelfth century. The Fourth Crusade and its consequences made it incurable. The Byzantine Empire had once covered a vast extent of territory in Europe and Asia, embracing a multi-racial but largely Greek-speaking society, with its administration and defence centralized in Constantinople. After the event of 1204 there was never any hope of reuniting the shattered fragments of that territory or of making Constantinople once again the hub of a unified Byzantine world, strong enough to withstand the simultaneous pressures from the Latin west and the Muslim east. The loss of territory to the crusaders meant also the loss of the resources and the manpower that went with it. The Latin conquest of Greece and the Greek islands therefore made the Turkish conquest of Asia Minor almost inevitable; and once Asia Minor, formerly the heartland of the empire, was lost, the conquest of Constantinople was only a matter of time. The astonishingly rapid advance of the Turks in eastern Europe in the fourteenth century demonstrates the pitiful weakness of Byzantium when confronted with the vitality of a vigorous new people. It was the Slavs and not the Greeks who at the end found the means and the will to put up some real, if ineffective, resistance to the Turks.

The tide might have been turned by a united effort of eastern and western Christendom. But this, for all the fond hopes of some of the last emperors, was never to be achieved. The memory of the Fourth Crusade and the continuing subjugation of much of their empire by the Latins reinforced the inherent prejudices of most Byzantines. The prejudices were no less strong on the Latin side; and there they were justified by the universal ideology of the papacy. The popes consistently regarded Byzantium as a lost sheep to be restored, by force if necessary, to the fold of Rome. They could not bring themselves to preach a crusade for the rescue of those whom they held to be in schism and in heresy; and they forced the Byzantines into an ever deeper and more desperate isolationism. It took the papacy a long time to observe the obvious truth that Constantinople and not Jerusalem was the focal point of Christianity in the east. Likewise, the Latin colonists in Greece looked to Rome, to Venice, to Genoa, or to Naples to protect and defend their interests. They too ignored the fact that they were living in a world whose natural and historical centre was Constantinople; and they drained away the wealth and strength of Byzantium to enrich their motherlands. What is remarkable about the end of the Byzantine Empire is that it did not come sooner, and that Byzantine society continued almost to the last to put forth new shoots of cultural and religious experience.

## Epilogue

Great and noble men often die as tragic invalids after long illnesses bravely borne. So it was with the Byzantine Empire. One after another limb of its body was affected until the heart, the city of Constantinople, could stand it no more. Some of its malady, as is often the case with men, was self-inflicted. But the worst of it was a creeping paralysis over which it had no control and for which there was no remedy. The divisive forces in its body politic, the social upheavals, the perennial conflicts of its ruling class, were symptoms of its struggle to master the disease. Outlying parts of the Byzantine world like Serbia had the good fortune to go down in a blaze of glory, at the Marica, at Kossovo, in battles which were the stuff of legend. The Byzantines were condemned to a more lingering death, which does not make for heroics. Only at the end, at Constantinople in May 1453, was there great heroism. But the songs which the Byzantines sang in their captivity were not heroic ballads. They were dirges and laments for the loss of their city and their world.

All that survived to remind them of their imperial past was their religion. It was their Orthodox faith and not their Hellenic philosophy that fortified them in their hours of need. A Greek under Turkish rule would enter his local church or monastery as one entering into a forgotten world of glory, where the paintings and icons would recall the peculiar yet familiar Byzantine blend of imperial and celestial mystery; where he would be surrounded by images of the church fathers dressed as Byzantine patriarchs, the warrior saints as Byzantine officers, Saints Constantine and Helena crowned and robed as emperor and empress, and the well-known figures of Christ, the Virgin and the saints still portrayed in the unchanging style which expressed the eternal truths of the spirit even in a changed world. If the fall of Constantinople severed the last tenuous link between Byzantium and the west, if thereafter the Christians in the Ottoman Empire clung more jealously than ever to their Orthodoxy and to their suspicion of the Latins, who can say that the western world was not to blame for having willed them into a spiritual alienation as the price of material help which never came?

# Note on further reading

An outline history of the period is given by G. Ostrogorsky, *History of the Byzantine State*, translated by Joan Hussey (2nd edn., Oxford, 1968). The most detailed narrative in English is by D. M. Nicol, *The Last Centuries of Byzantium, 1261–1453* (London, 1972). The relevant chapters of the *Cambridge Medieval History*, IV, 1: *The Byzantine Empire* (Cambridge, 1966), should also be consulted.

Monographs and specialized studies of the reigns of certain emperors are contained in the following: D. J. Geanakoplos, *Emperor Michael Palaeologus and the West, 1258–1282* (Cambridge, Mass., 1959); Angeliki E. Laiou, *Constantinople and the Latins: The Foreign Policy of Andronicus II* (Cambridge, Mass., 1972); Ursula V. Bosch, *Kaiser Andronikos III. Palaiologos* (Amsterdam, 1965); D. M. Nicol, *The Byzantine Family of Kantakouzenos (Cantacuzenus): A Genealogical and Prosopographical Study,* Dumbarton Oaks Studies, XI (Washington, D.C., 1968); O. Halecki, *Un Empereur de Byzance à Rome* (Warsaw, 1930); J. W. Barker, *Manuel II Palaeologus (1391–1425): A study in late Byzantine statesmanship* (New Brunswick, N.J., 1968).

On the church councils of Lyons (1274) and Florence (1439) the standard works are: B. Roberg, *Die Union zwischen der griechischen und der lateinischen Kirche auf dem II. Konzil von Lyon* (Bonn, 1964) and J. Gill, *The Council of Florence* (Cambridge, 1959). An account of the structure and theology of the late Byzantine church and its relations with the western church is given in Book 1 of S. Runciman, *The Great Church in Captivity: A Study of the Patriarchate of Constantinople from the Eve of the Turkish Conquest to the Greek War of Independence* (Cambridge, 1968); and for the special relationship between church and state in Byzantium see S. Runciman, *The Byzantine Theocracy* (Cambridge, 1977). An account of Byzantine monasticism will be found in D. M. Nicol, *Meteora: The Rock Monasteries of Thessaly* (2nd edn., London, 1975); and the best approach to an understanding of hesychasm is through the works of J. Meyendorff, *Introduction à l'étude de Grégoire Palamas* (Paris, 1959), translated as *A Study of Gregory Palamas* by G. Lawrence (London, 1965), and *Byzantine Theology: Historical Trends and Doctrinal Themes* (New York, 1974).

Accounts of the intellectual and cultural life of the period will be found in S. Runciman, *The Last Byzantine Renaissance* (Cambridge, 1970) and S. Runciman, *Byzantine Style and Civilization* (Harmondsworth, 1975). For more detailed study of particular topics in this field, see: H.-G. Beck, *Theodoros Metochites. Die Krise des byzantinischen Weltbildes im 14 Jahrhundert* (Munich, 1952); F. Masai, *Plêthon et le Platonisme de Mistra* (Paris, 1956); B. Tatakis, *La Philosophie byzantine*, in *Histoire de la Philosophie*, edited by E. Bréhier, fasc. suppl. II (Paris, 1959); P. Underwood (ed.), *The Kariye Djami*, IV (New York, 1975).

There is no satisfactory study on the central and provincial administration of the empire in these centuries (except for the work of Lj. Maksimović published in Belgrade in 1972, which is in Serbo-Croat). But some information can be found in L.-P. Raybaud, *Le gouvernment et l'administration centrale de l'empire byzantin sous les premiers Paléologues (1258–1354)* (Paris, 1968). On social, economic and agrarian problems the following are particularly useful: G. Ostrogorsky, *Pour l'histoire de la féodalité byzantine*, and *Quelques problèmes d'histoire de la paysannerie byzantine* (Brussels, 1954 and 1956); A. E. Laiou-Thomadakis, *Peasant Society in the Late Byzantine Empire: A Social and Demographic Study* (Princeton, N.J., 1977); D. A. Zakythinos, *Crise monétaire et crise économique à Byzance du XIII^e au XV^e siècle* (Athens, 1948); P. Charanis, *Social, Economic and Political Life in the Byzantine Empire: Collected Studies* (London, 1973).

Regional studies of the separatist or provincial states are: M. Angold, *A Byzantine Government in Exile: Government and Society Under the Laskarids of Nicaea (1204–1261)* (Oxford, 1975); W. Miller, *Trebizond. The Last Greek Empire* (London, 1926); D. M. Nicol, *The Despotate of Epiros* (Oxford, 1957); D. A. Zakythinos, *Le Despotat grec de Morée (1262–1460)* (2 vols, 2nd edn, London, 1975). Also useful is A. E. Vacalopoulos, *Origins of the Greek Nation, 1204–1461* (New Brunswick, N.J., 1970). The only serious study of Mistra and its civilization is in Russian, by I. P. Medvedev, *Mistra* (Leningrad, 1973). On Thessalonica, O. Tafrali, *Thessalonique au XIV^e siècle* (Paris, 1913) is much out of date but still interesting.

Late Byzantine relations with the western world are analysed in the two studies by D. J. Geanakoplos, *Byzantine East and Latin West: Two Worlds of Christendom in Middle Ages and Renaissance* (Oxford, 1956), and *Interaction of the 'Sibling' Byzantine and Western Cultures in the Middle Ages and Italian Renaissance* (New Haven and London, 1976). For the thirteenth century see especially S. Runciman, *The Sicilian Vespers: A History of the Mediterranean World in the Late Thirteenth Century* (Cambridge, 1958). The effect of the later crusades on Byzantium is discussed in: S. Runciman, *A History of the Crusades*, III (Cambridge, 1954);

K. M. Setton (ed.), *A History of the Crusades,* II: *The Later Crusades, 1198-1311*, edited by R. L. Wolff and H. W. Hazard (Philadelphia, 1962); III: *The Fourteenth and Fifteenth Centuries*, edited by H. W. Hazard (Madison, 1975); A. S. Atiya, *The Crusade of Nicopolis* (London, 1934); O. Halecki, *The Crusade of Varna* (New York, 1943). See also K. M. Setton, *The Papacy and the Levant (1204–1511),* I: *The Thirteenth and Fourteenth Centuries* (Philadelphia, 1976).

The history of the Latin Empire of Constantinople and western colonization in Byzantium is contained in the following works: W. Miller, *The Latins in the Levant: A History of Frankish Greece, 1204–1566* (London, 1908); J. Longnon, *L'empire latin de Constantinople et la principauté de Morée* (Paris, 1949); F. Thiriet, *La Romanie vénitienne au moyen âge* (Paris, 1959). See also: A. Bon, *La Morée franque. Recherches historiques, topographiques et archéologiques sur la principauté d'Achaie (1204–1430)* (2 vols, Paris, 1969); W. Miller, *Essays on the Latin Orient* (Cambridge, 1921).

Especially valuable for the history of the northern neighbours of Byzantium is D. Obolensky, *The Byzantine Commonwealth: Eastern Europe 500–1453* (London, 1971).

The rise of the Ottoman Empire, The Turkish conquest of Byzantium and the fall of Constantinople are well covered in a number of books, of which the following are perhaps the most important: C. Cahen, *Pre-Ottoman Turkey* (London, 1968); H. Inalcik, *The Ottoman Empire: The Classical Age 1300–1600* (London, 1973); H. A. Gibbons, *The Foundation of the Ottoman Empire: A History of the Osmanlis up to the Death of Bayezid I, 1300–1403* (Oxford, 1916); P. Lemerle, *L'Emirat d'Aydin, Byzance et l'Occident. Recherches sur 'La geste d'Umur Pacha'* (Paris, 1957); S. Runciman, *The Fall of Constantinople, 1453* (Cambridge, 1965); S. Vryonis, *The Decline of Medieval Hellenism in Asia Minor and the Process of Islamization from the Eleventh through the Fifteenth Century* (Berkeley, Los Angeles, London, 1971); P. Wittek, *The Rise of the Ottoman Empire,* Royal Asiatic Society Monographs, 23 (London, 1938).

Finally, much valuable material is contained in the *Collected Studies* of the following authors published by Variorum Reprints, London: P. Charanis, *Social, Economic and Political Life in the Byzantine Empire* (1973); J. Meyendorff, *Byzantine Hesychasm: Historical, Theological and Social Problems* (1974); D. M. Nicol, *Byzantium: Its Ecclesiastical History and Relations with the Western World* (1972); D. Obolensky, *Byzantium and the Slavs* (1971); K. M. Setton, *Europe and the Levant in the Middle Ages and the Renaissance* (1974); S. Vryonis, *Byzantium: Its Internal History and Relations with the Muslim World* (1971).

# Chronological table of main events

1204 Capture of Constantinople by the Fourth Crusade.
1259 Battle of Pelagonia.
1261 Recovery of Constantinople and restoration of Byzantine Empire: Michael VIII Palaiologos.
1266 Charles of Anjou King of the Two Sicilies.
1274 Second Council of Lyons.
1282 Sicilian Vespers (March). Death of Michael VIII (December). Andronikos II Palaiologos.
1299 Byzantine treaty with Serbia (Stephen Milutin).
1302 Byzantines defeated by Osman.
1303 Catalan Company arrive in Constantinople.
1307 Byzantine treaty with Bulgaria.
1311 Catalans capture Athens.
1321 First civil war: Andronikos II against Andronikos III.
1325 Coronation of Andronikos III as co-emperor.
1326 Osmanlis capture Prousa; Orchan succeeds Osman.
1328 Abdication of Andronikos II.
1330 Battle of Velbužd: Serbians defeat Bulgarians.
1331 Osmanlis capture Nicaea.
1333 First treaty between Byzantines and Osmanlis (Ottomans).
1333 Thessaly restored to Byzantine rule.
1340 Epiros restored to Byzantine rule.
1341 Death of Andronikos III. Second civil war: John V Palaiologos against John VI Cantacuzene.
1342 Zealot revolution in Thessalonica (until 1350).
1346 Stephen Dušan of Serbia crowned emperor.
1347 John VI Cantacuzene enters Constantinople as emperor; end of second civil war. Black Death in Constantinople.
1348 Serbian occupation of Thessaly and Epiros.
1348–9 Byzantine–Genoese war.
1349 Manuel Cantacuzene Despot of the Morea.
1351 Hesychast council in Constantinople.
1352 War between Matthew Cantacuzene and John V Palaiologos.
1354 Gallipoli occupied by Turks (March). John V Palaiologos enters Constantinople; John VI Cantacuzene abdicates (December).
1355 Death of Stephen Dušan (December).
1362 Death of Orchan; Murad I sultan.

1366 John V visits Hungary. Amadeo of Savoy recaptures Gallipoli.
1369 John V to Rome.
1371 Battle of the Marica river: Serbians defeated by Turks.
1376–9 Andronikos IV emperor in Constantinople.
1383 John VI Cantacuzene dies in the Morea.
1382–7 Manuel Palaiologos emperor in Thessalonica.
1385 Turkish capture of Sofia.
1387 Turkish capture of Thessalonica.
1389 Turkish capture of Trnovo. Battle of Kossovo (June): Serbians defeated by Turks. Death of Murad I; Bajezid I sultan.
1390 John VII emperor in Constantinople. Turkish capture of Philadelphia.
1391 Death of John V; Manuel II emperor.
1393 Turkish conquest and annexation of Bulgaria.
1394 Turkish blockade of Constantinople (until 1402).
1396 Crusade of Nikopolis.
1399 Manuel II to Italy.
1400–1403 Manuel II in France and England.
1402 Battle of Ankara: Turks defeated by Mongols (July). Capture of sultan Bajezid I.
1403 Treaty between Byzantines and Turks: Byzantine recovery of Thessalonica etc. War between Bajezid's sons.
1410 Suleiman defeated by Musa.
1413 Musa defeated by Mehmed I.
1421 Death of Mehmed I: Murad II sultan.
1422 Siege of Constantinople by Turks.
1423 Thessalonica ceded to Venice.
1425 Death of Manuel II (July): John VIII emperor.
1430 Thessalonica captured by Murad II.
1437 John VIII to Italy.
1438–9 Council of Ferrara/Florence: union of churches (July 1439).
1439 Turkish capture of Smederevo.
1440 Turkish capture of Belgrade.
1443–4 Crusade of Varna.
1448 Death of John VIII (October).
1449 Constantine XI crowned emperor at Mistra.
1451 Death of Murad II (February): Mehmed II sultan.
1452 Union of churches proclaimed in Constantinople (December).
1453 Siege and capture of Constantinople by Mehmed II (29 May).
1456 Turkish capture of Athens.
1460 Turkish capture of Mistra.
1461 Turkish capture of Trebizond.

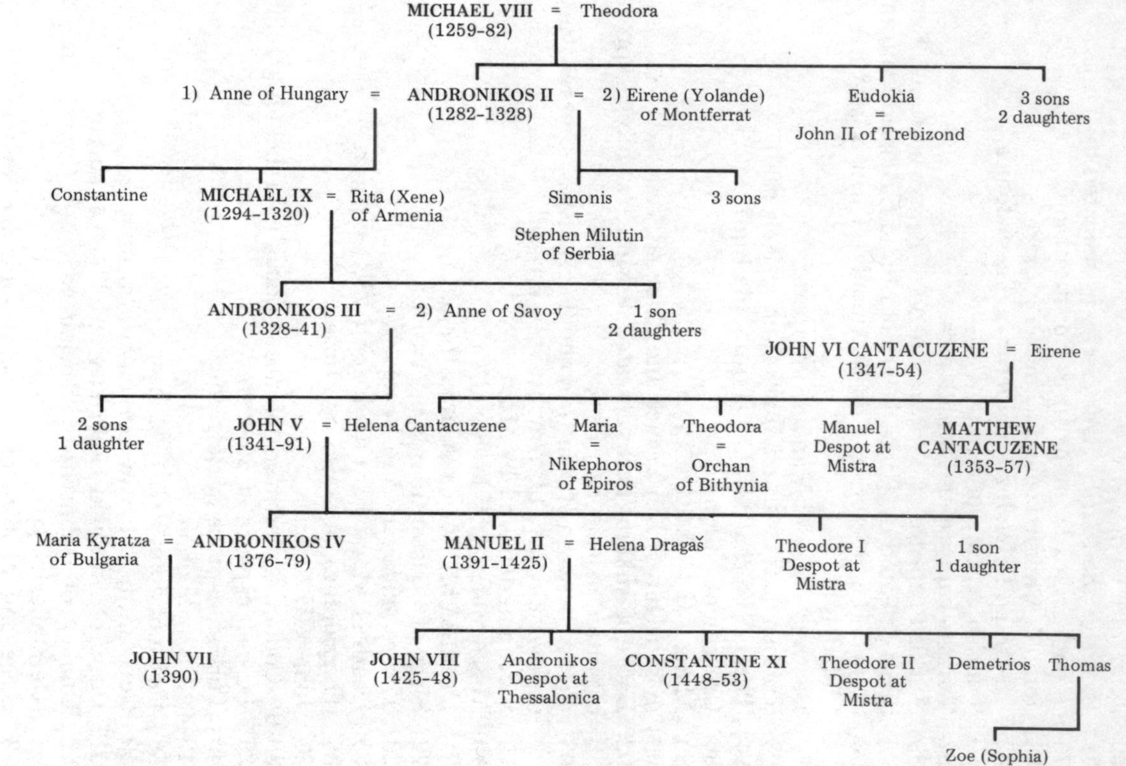


THE DYNASTY OF PALAIOLOGOS

# INDEX